Personal Proofs

Experiential Evidences for the Existence of God (and Spiritual Senses)

Frederick A. Swarts

Hudson MacArthur Publishers

Copyright © 2020 by Hudson MacArthur Publishers, Inc.

All rights reserved. No part of this book may be reproduced or transmitted in any form or any means electronic or mechanical, including photocopying, recording, internet transmittal, or any information storage or retrieval system, without prior written permission from the publisher, except in the case of brief quotations embodied in reviews or in critical articles. For information, address Hudson MacArthur Publishers, P.O. Box 1008, Gouldsboro, PA 18424.

ISBN 978-0-9675946-4-4
Ebook ISBN 978-0-9675946-5-1

Published in the United States by
Hudson MacArthur Publishers, Inc.
P.O. Box 1008, Gouldsboro, PA 18424

Cover design/image: Rod Cameron

To Lourdes

Contents

Preface   vii

Belief and Non-Belief   1
    A growing tide of non-belief in the age of science?   5
    Navigating the God/no God enigma   7
    Dark night of the soul   12
    The proofs   13

Precognitive Dreams   17
    Pier-Angelo dream   20
    Savannah dream   24

Personal Experiences with Spiritual Senses   27
    The Nevada experience   29
    Meditation and the "peak experience"   33
    Meditation possession   37
    Hearing a voice   40

Synchronicity   43
    Savannah, Georgia Two   49
    Airplane coincidences   52
    Batch Hall, Cornell University   56
    Borders   58
    Three in a photo   60

Prayer Experiences   63
    Rain   65
    Three dreams   68
    The spiritual healing   70

Spiritual Experiences of Others   73
    Trusted sources   75
    Colleagues' experiences   77
    Lourdes   80

Notes   87

About the Author   91

Preface

This book was originally drafted more than a decade ago. Always on my mind, never completed until now, the text actually hasn't changed much in all those years. Some research studies have been added to supplement background information, but the essence remains the same. After all, this work is mostly an accumulation of my personal experiences, ones that buttress the hypothesis of a transcendent being and preternatural faculties of perception.

These are not images of Jesus appearing in the shape of a piece of burnt toast. These are a selection of often-intricate experiences that I believe you will find intrinsically captivating and thought-provoking. These also are not the product of someone conditioned or indoctrinated to imagine spiritual experiences; I am a scientist by trade and a number of these occurred when I didn't believe in God. And my basic nature remains that of a skeptical scientist. But a "skeptic," in the best sense of the term, is not just a questioning person, but also one open to new data, new experiences, things that might change one's paradigm. Or, as Hamlet said to Horatio, "There are more things in heaven and earth, than are dreamt of in your philosophy."

There is a companion text that was written concomitantly with this original draft and which also was near completion more than a decade ago. This "Part II," tentatively titled *God and Today's Science: Musings on Evolution and Nature*, deals not with personal spiritual experiences but evidences of God gained from a study of nature, the issue of the (not-so) "hidden God." In also addressing evolutionary theory, a focus of my doctoral studies, this yet-unfinished work provides a clearly delineated overview of the topic—one often obfuscated in popular writings and high school textbooks—and then addresses key convergences and divergences from religious belief. I hope that I will not take another decade to put the finishing touches on that text.

The word "proofs" in the title of this present work is used synonymously with "evidences," a common rendering of this noun. It shouldn't be confused with philosophical proofs of God's existence. And, although some conflate the meanings, it shouldn't be confused with the verb "prove." Although they come from the same Latin root, the meanings are very different, and I do not want the readers to think that I am presumptuously claiming to prove anything, neither God's existence nor the reality of spiritual senses. The fact is no amount of evidence, even extraordinary in nature, can prove any hypothesis one hundred percent; as readers know, evidences can only support or negate a hypothesis. But what one can do is amass evidences, and that is what this book is about. These are evidences, "proofs," that I experienced and find confirming on a "personal" basis.

Richard Dawkins' stated purpose of writing *The God Delusion* was "if this book works as I intend, religious readers who open it will be atheists when they put it down." My purpose is a mirror image. If this book works as I intend, readers will be more open-minded toward the data provided through religious phenomena, and atheists, when they put this work down, will think twice about dismissing religious experiences out of hand. I hope that in this I am successful

PERSONAL

PROOFS

Belief and Non-Belief

At the time of the winter solstice, let reason prevail. There are no gods, no devils, no angels, no heaven or hell. There is only our natural world. Religion is just myth and superstition that hardens hearts and enslaves minds.

The above words made their debut in December 1996 on an engraved sign posted in the Wisconsin State Capitol in Madison. Crafted by Anne Nicol Gaylor, founder of a nonprofit dedicated to "freedom from religion," the quote has been displayed every year since in the rotunda there. The same message was soon spread by enthusiasts to other government venues, and in December 2008 garnered national attention when signs were placed in the grand marble hallways of the Washington State Capitol and in the rotunda of the Illinois State Capitol, reflecting a perspective discordant with nearby nativity scenes. The Mississippi State Capitol in Jackson; the Rhode Island Capitol in Province; the Michigan Capitol in Lansing; and the Loudown County Courthouse in Leesburg have featured these words, as have many other government buildings.

In June 2013, perhaps the nation's first atheist monument on government property occurred when the American Atheists unveiled a granite bench to their nonbelief in God in front of the Bradford County Courthouse in Florida.

Belief in a God, spirit, or life force has been denigrated as the realm of the ignorant through more scholarly means as well.

In his 2006 work *The God Delusion*, renowned atheist/evolutionary biologist Richard Dawkins (self-identifying as an agnostic, but 6.9 on his 7-point "strong theist"/"strong atheist" spectrum[1]) argues that religious beliefs stem from childhood indoctrination and poor education. Others trace belief in God to a residual flaw in the brain. Humans are wired that way, claims Bruce Hood, as an artifact of a once-important evolutionarily adaptation. Hood, a professor of developmental psychology specializing in cognitive neuroscience, contends supernatural beliefs aided human survival in the past and now remain programmed into our brains from birth. As children grow up, they become more rational, asserts Hood, but these "illogical supernatural beliefs" are so fundamentally hardwired that they persist nonetheless.[2]

Lack of belief in a personal God is particularly high among scientists, or at least prominently recognized American and (British) Commonwealth scientists. In an oft-cited 1998 study published in the journal *Nature*, researchers reported nearly universal rejection of belief in God among members of the National Academy of Sciences (NAS), with only 7 percent professing belief.[3] The NAS was established by an Act of Congress (signed by President Abraham Lincoln) over one hundred and fifty years ago; its membership consists of U.S. citizens who have demonstrated excellence in science and original research, and who have gone through a rigorous process of nomination, extensive vetting, and election. This is a distinguished and elite group; around two hundred members have received Nobel prizes. In this 1998 survey of NAS members, almost three-fourths of the scientists rejected the transcendent, with the rest mostly placing themselves in the category of "doubt or agnosticism." Biological scientists were especially non-religious, with only 5.5 percent affirming belief in God and 7.1 percent embracing immortality.

The British counterpart, the Royal Society, has a similarly overwhelming number of its members rejecting belief in a personal God or that consciousness survives death.[4] Formed in 1660, the Royal Society (termed in its Second Royal Charter of 1663 as "the Royal Society of London for Improving Natural Knowledge") is a select Fellowship of about sixteen hundred eminent scientists from the United Kingdom and the Commonwealth. In a survey published in 2013, based on a 7-point, Likert-type scale (1 = strongly disagree, 7 = strongly agree), 78 percent of the responding Fellows strongly disagreed (answer 1 or 2) with the statement that God exists ("I believe that there is a strong likelihood that a supernatural being such as God exists or has existed") and a staggering 86.6 percent disagreed with the statement that there is a personal God ("I believe in a personal God, that is one who takes interests in individuals, hears and answers prayers, is concerned with sin and transgressions, and passes judgement"). Only 8.1 percent of the scientists polled strongly agreed (answer 6 or 7) with the view that God exists and merely 5.3 percent expressed belief in a personal God. Belief in consciousness surviving death ("I believe that when we physically die, our subjective consciousness, or some part of it, survives") was at the level of just 8.1 percent strongly agreeing (answer 6 or 7) with that statement, with 85.6 percent strongly disagreeing (answer 1 or 2).

Of course, the above survey data doesn't reflect the views of scientists in general, but rather the perspective of an exclusive group of eminent scientists in particular countries (the United States and Commonwealth nations). A 2009 survey of U.S.-based scientists belonging to the American Association for the Advancement of Science (AAAS), an international scientific society with over one hundred and twenty thousand members, revealed a much more accepting attitude toward belief in God. This survey by the Pew Research Center found 51 percent of the

American scientists polled expressed either belief in God—33 percent ("I believe in God")—or in a universal spirit or higher power—18 percent ("I don't believe in God, but I do believe in a universal spirit or higher power").[5] A 2015 worldwide survey of religion and science by researchers at Rice University showed that more than half of the scientists in Italy, India, and Turkey self-identify as religious.[6]

And certainly profession of faith in a deity is common among the public at large in most nations, including the United States and European nations. Three Pew Research Center surveys of Americans, conducted between 2006 and 2017, show belief in God or a universal spirit or higher power to range from 95 percent to 89 percent, about nine out of every ten people.[7] And while secularism is common in Western Europe, with some countries having less believers than believers, various surveys still show 65 percent (2018 Pew Research Center survey) to 77 percent (Eurobarometer Poll 2010) of the general public in the European Union to believe in God, a higher power, or a spirit or life force.[8]

Yet, non-belief in a God, spirit, and an afterlife is anything but a rare phenomenon. While the number of atheists in North America, Latin America, Africa, and the Middle East remain relatively small in number, sociologists Ariela Keysar and Juhem Navarro-Rivera claim 7 percent of the world's population has embraced atheism or agnosticism—about five hundred million people.[9] Likewise, the earlier-noted 2010 Eurobarometer Poll revealed that one in five Europeans reject belief in a spirit, God, or life force, rising to one in four in the United Kingdom and four in ten in France. In 2016, a survey of Norwegians showed, for the first time, more non-believers than believers.[10]

A growing tide of non-belief in the age of science?

Do the polls of eminent scientists, and signs placed in the U.S. public square, reflect a growing tide of non-belief in God? Is the view that science and religion are in conflict something shared by increasing numbers, or a myth, perhaps fostered by those who see religion as outdated and delusional superstition? Quite frankly, I have no idea. Survey data itself only reflects what people are willing to divulge, and religion is one of those personal and emotion-laden topics that can yield distorted results.

In this age of science and easy access to information, certainly many scientifically informed people do perceive a conflict between current scientific knowledge and religious belief. Neuroscience, some surmise, is well on the way to debunking religious experiences as simply a product of the brain, placing such in the same category as hallucinations of leprechauns and fairies caused by brain injury, drugs, oxygen depletion, physical trauma, or mental illness. Evolutionary science has offered an alternative to creation by a supreme being. Physics offers a non-theistic explanation for the origin of the universe. Psychologists postulate belief in an afterlife as a means to address fear of death or loss of loved ones. For many, media exposure of religious charlatans, the knowledge that certain religious superstitions or illogical beliefs do conflict with established scientific principles, and reflection on incidents of intolerance or immoral practices within the history of religions further positions faith in a supreme being as archaic in the modern age.

If there is a modern dethroning of God and boldness in asserting such non-belief then the ascendency of evolutionary theory would be pegged as a contributing factor. While many religious adherents seamlessly juxtapose belief in God with evolutionary theory, others look at evolutionary theory as if it posits an either-or dichotomy—either evolution is true or the existence of God is true. One famous evolutionist who embraced this view was Julian Huxley, who stated in "The New Divinity" (in his book *Essays of a Humanist*):

> *There is no separate supernatural realm: all phenomena are part of one natural process of evolution. . . . God is a hypothesis constructed by man to help him understand what existence is all about. Today the god hypothesis has ceased to be scientifically tenable . . . and its abandonment often brings a deep sense of relief.*

Thus, we find ourselves at a point in history where many biologists, physicists, psychologists, and other leading scientists and academics readily dismiss belief in God as the realm of the ignorant and programmed. When such a revered figure as physicist Stephen Hawking speaks, people listen. In his final book, completed after his death, he is unambiguous: "It's my view that there is no God. No one created the universe…I think belief in the afterlife is just wishful thinking. There is no reliable evidence for it, and it flies in the face of everything we know in science."[11]

Reflecting the earlier-mentioned views of biologist Richard Dawkins (childhood indoctrination, realm of the ignorant) and psychologist Bruce Hood (residual flaw in the brain), comedian and television host Bill Maher takes it a step further, seriously intoning that "religion is a neurological disorder," afflicting the unenlightened. Or, as the late Robert M. Pirsig (*Zen and the Art of Motorcycle Maintenance*) stated, "When one person suffers from a delusion, it is called insanity. When many people suffer from a delusion it is called Religion."

With so many considering belief in God a neurological condition or product of indoctrination and ignorance and superstition, it's not too hard to speculate that only the sheer number of religious adherents in the world has precluded belief in God and spirit from being listed in the *Diagnostic and Statistical Manual of Mental Disorders*.

Consequently, despite the fact that innumerable people have had spiritual experiences throughout history, both profound and mundane, and in diverse religious disciplines, those events rarely serve as data for an objective analysis in the scientific community. Instead, treated as if the projections of a weak, ill, or programmed mind, they are summarily dismissed, as if claimed sightings of the Easter Bunny.

But, given that such experiences address the ultimate question—how one answers the query of whether or not God exists is a major determinate factor in how one lives his or her life—would it not be better to treat such experiences as data for insight into that life-altering answer?

Navigating the God/no God enigma

Richard Dawkins writes in *The God Delusion* that faith "is usually some form of childhood indoctrination." He talks of "dyed-in-the-wool faith-heads" who "are immune to argument," whereas atheists are "open-minded people" or those "whose native intelligence is strong enough to overcome" such childhood brainwashing.

This may be Dawkins' experience. It has not been mine, neither in my personal life or among many of the highly educated religious people that I know. Many, like myself, actually moved from an earlier atheism/agnosticism to belief based exactly on being open-minded—that is, being opened-minded about reports of religious experiences and their own first-hand experiences.

Comedian Seth MacFarlane (creator of *Family Guy* and *American Dad!*) proclaims "I do not believe in God. I'm an atheist. I consider myself a critical thinker." He may find it fascinating "that in the 21st century most people still believe" in God, but what fascinates me is that people who consider themselves open-minded and critical thinkers so readily dismiss the personal and religious experiences of others, or injudiciously pigeonhole great swaths of humanity as indoctrinated, closed-minded, "dyed-in-the-wool faith-heads."

The core of this book deal with my own personal experiences that helped me navigate the God/No God question.

As a biological scientist, for much of my life I fit in well with those rejecting belief in God. For me, humans were just another primate, albeit an intelligent one. Religious believers were living in the dark ages of mythology and superstition, hanging onto belief as a crutch, in spite of the revolutionary advance of science and human knowledge. When individuals would confide in me about their experiences seeing "spirits" or having "out-of-body" experiences, I either looked at them as weak-minded or psychologically troubled people, or more commonly, just disregarded their experiences as not worth my time to even contemplate. I put them, or their experiences, in a neat, little, mental box and set it aside because such didn't fit in my paradigm.

"Zombie Science" is a term coined by Jonathan Wells for explanations for phenomena that are inconsistent with evidence, and thus empirically dead, yet embraced because they comfortably fit within a materialistic philosophy. Wells, who holds a Ph.D. in molecular and cell biology from the University of California-Berkeley and a Ph.D. in religious studies from Yale, advocates for following evidence wherever it leads, not trying to shoehorn it into a materialistic explanation. Zombie

Science might be a somewhat apt descriptor for my mindset at the time, not necessarily in terms of clinging to explanations inconsistent with evidence but certainly in excluding apriori all but materialistic ones.

Today, I stand convinced about the existence of God and an inner spiritual essence in humans. To a large extent, this transformation is tied to opening my mind a crack to the possibility of spiritual phenomena and then encountering an entire realm of evidences that I'd previously ignored. Catalogued in this book are a number of my own experiences and a few of those of close associates. I will not detail any of the myriad testimonies recorded throughout history: what has proved so easy for me to dismiss when relayed second-hand I couldn't simply explain away in terms of events in my own life.

Of course, investigating the transcendent via religious experiences is far removed from inquiries into the natural world via the logical-scientific method of inquiry, which has been so powerfully employed by physics, astronomy, biology, chemistry, and similar domains. Representing an altogether different dimension of human perception, an individual's personal, subjective, mystical experience is resistant to many research methodologies. It is not replicable, defies precision measurement and validation, and cannot be stimulated to occur as part of an experiment.

Yet, the universality of such phenomena, in virtually all human societies and throughout recorded history, also means these experiences cannot, or at least in my view should not, be readily dismissed. Even renowned scientists have allowed for the transcendent. Einstein, by no means a believer in a personal God, nonetheless reported that a "cosmic religious feeling" inspired his reflections on the order and harmony of the universe.[12] Astronomer Fred Hoyle credited a dramatic revelatory insight with his solving a particularly difficult quantum mechanical problem.[13] Hoyle further conjectured that a "superintelligence" acting at the quantum level can implant thoughts and insights into the human brain; other scientists likewise posit that the formulation of scientific theories can be aided by mystical insights.[14]

Nonetheless, experiential data dealing with mystical experiences is not only routinely disregarded by scientists in their personal lives, but also their professional lives, where the *unreality* of God and spirit seems to be the working assumption in today's scientific paradigm. For a scientist to first take for granted that there is no God, and then speculate why people have such superstitions—that such stems from a flaw in the brain, that it was passed down as an evolutionary adaptation, that it is an artifact of an effort by the brain to look for meaningful patterns, that people cling to delusions as a crutch—is to prejudice their research and ignore a great deal of data. One could just as well start with the premise that the wealth of religious/spiritual phenomena is explained on the basis of their being a God and spirit.

Of course, ultimately the question of God's existence is one that each person must grapple with individually. For some, it is a straightforward process: They have experiences of God and/or an incorporeal reality. For others, it can be considerably more challenging. While philosophical/rational arguments or proofs for the existence of God abound, such are not very satisfying for most people. It is my perspective that the experiential offers more convincing evidences for most individuals personally. Of course, there are limitations in spiritual phenomena as source material—such experiences can be quite unreliable as guidance for one's life. But as evidence of the transcendent, they can be powerful.

Individuals guided by sincerity, openness, and effort should be in a good position to gain insight into this issue of God versus non-God. In Hinduism, the term yoga connotes ways to divine realization, with four principal paths recognized: the way to God through knowledge (jnana yoga), love (bhakti yoga), work (karma yoga), and psychophysical exercises (raja yoga). Different spiritual types might use different disciplines. My own course utilized aspects of each pathway, with greater emphasis on knowledge. My intellectual pursuits—largely grappling with the philosophical insights from Rev. Sun Myung Moon and his work *The Divine Principle*—provided a framework for understanding the experiences gained via the other three methods.

In my case, as a mid-twenties evolutionary biologist and agnostic (somewhat north of six on Dawkins seven-point scale), I made a personal determination to devote three years of my life to tackling the fundamental question of God's existence. I remember hoping that my quest would be in vain, thus freeing me from the restrictions I envisioned a life of faith would entail. But I'd had some pretty unusual experiences that opened me up to the possibility of something "spiritual," and I felt an obligation to undertake a quest to at least try and tackle this ultimate question. And I had another motive: If a personal God actually existed, and was a being with heart and feeling, then whom am I to cause additional pain with my actions? In this quest, I left my comfort zone and undertook tasks that challenged me emotionally and physically. Many of the experiences in this book were a byproduct of operating in such uncomfortable situations.

It is my recommendation that each reader reflects open-mindedly on his or her own experiences that might reveal the presence of God, as well as probe trusted friends, family members, and colleagues for their experiences. This book offers a framework for categorizing the diversity of such events. One likewise might also find it helpful to put in writing the relevant phenomena they encounter. For one, we are living in an increasingly secularized society where present stimulation can dull remembrances of past incidents, no matter how intense such were at the time. But even for believers, there is a key reason to record personal experiences in some fixed form: the phenomenon known as the "dark night of the soul."

Dark night of the soul

The term "dark night of the soul" is a metaphor for a period in a believer's life when there is a sense of spiritual loneliness and separation from God. During this spiritual crisis, a person who believes in God and has a strong prayer life may suddenly feel distant from God, as if abandoned, or may feel his or her prayer life is difficult, unrewarding—or dead. One may come to doubt the very existence of God. Some dark nights of the soul can be very extensive. In the 18th century, St. Paul of the Cross claimed such a dark night that lasted 45 years, although he eventually came out of this desolate period.

One of the most notable dark nights of the soul was that experienced by Mother Teresa of Calcutta. A devoted Roman Catholic nun for seventy years and the founder of Missionaries of Charity, Mother Teresa lived a life of service to the most destitute and desperate people. In 1979 she received the Nobel Peace Prize, and in 2003 she was beatified by Pope John Paul II. Yet, letters released after her death in 1997 showed that she spent most of her life of faith suffering a dark night of the soul.

A series of mystical experiences that began on September 10, 1946—in which Mother Theresa claimed, without any doubt, that she heard Jesus' voice, conversed with him, and received her mission—was followed by nearly a half-century of deep spiritual pain and a feeling of the lack of God's presence, starting shortly after beginning her service to the poor in Calcutta in 1948. Apparently, other than during a five-week break in 1959 (shortly after the death of Pope Pius XII), this dark night of the soul never abated until near the end of her life.

The letters of Teresa record her spiritual "darkness," "torture," "loneliness," and "dryness." She continued her life of faith and work—her Missionaries of Charity would spread to more than five hundred missions and one hundred countries—but she recognized that her inner state didn't coincide with her public face. At one point, she confided to an advisor: "I spoke as if my very heart was in love with God—tender, personal love. . . . If you were [there], you would have said, 'What hypocrisy.'" To her, it was a form of Hell, where she could not feel God's love, only experience silence and emptiness. Finally, according to Franciscan Friar Father Benedict Groeschel, "the darkness left" near the end of her life.

My own encounter with such a dark night of the soul was much briefer. F. Scott Fitzgerald wrote, "In a real dark night of the soul it is always three o'clock in the morning." For me, it was three o'clock in the morning for over three months. Despite the previous occurrence of many of the personal spiritual experiences recorded in this book, I found myself in a state where my prayers were dead, and I couldn't feel God's presence. I played my spiritual experiences over in my head; they had no power to bring God alive in my life. I felt...nothing. Profound experiences that once moved me to great passion were like far distant events that had happened to someone else. And then, just as suddenly as it had appeared, the dark night of the soul lifted. What sustained me during this period was remembering well the substance of the personal experiences even if they lacked an emotional punch.

The proofs

In this book are chronicled a number of my personal experiences that support the view that there is a personal God and/or a spiritual dimension to people. I have added a few reports from close contacts whom I trust deeply. Many of the collected accounts I believe to be quite enlightening and convincing.

However, I surmise that to a neutral observer none of the experiences taken individually, no matter how special, constitute definitive proofs of God or spirit. After all, I had many of these experiences, over many years, before I myself felt that the only conclusion was that there must a personal God. It is not an easy concept for a nonbeliever to accept. And even after arriving to this affirmation, I continued to question my verdict even as I continued to accumulate additional confirming experiences.

After all, when talking about a singular event, one can speak of coincidences and mathematical probabilities, of selective memory, of brain neurochemistry and hallucinations. But when taken cumulatively, with many varied experiences spread out through diverse categories (spiritual senses, precognitive dreams, improbable coincidences, etc.), all being perceived by someone who was standing on the atheist side of the spectrum during many of the experiences, then this is grounds to reconsider one's position of unbelief. Add to this the accounts of trusted friends and colleagues and one finds significant support for belief in God and spiritual senses. For that neutral observer mentioned above, I would expect that the cumulative data being presented here would draw him or her to the same conclusion. And this is without considering the extraordinary history of religious experiences, showing the phenomena to be unremarkable in the sense of being ubiquitous.

There is a certain disquietude in realizing that many scientists appear to automatically discount spiritual experiences as a source of genuine data. And it's not as if they are proposing non-existence of a supreme being as simply a hypothesis to guide research, but more as if a fundamental axiom from which they can then propose reasons why people have such false beliefs and illusionary experiences.

Such scientists disingenuously cloak their arguments in the imprimatur of science, but they are soon leaping beyond scientific facts into speculation. Particularly galling is the use of impossible-to-prove, but nice sounding, social-evolutionary scenarios: human groups that were predisposed to falsely believe in deities had a greater chance of surviving than those that didn't believe; humans evolved a brain that not only looked for patterns for survival but invented the psychologically useful pattern of belief in a God and an afterlife; the cooperative needs of society required evolution of a brain where one's behavior is regulated by an omnipresent and omniscient deity who must be obeyed.

Thus, we are at a stage where non-belief is the prevailing paradigm in much of science, and those professing religious experiences find themselves viewed as superstitious, illogical, and ignorant by the intelligentsia. Perhaps this is why two graduate students in science who opened up to me about their spiritual experiences (one an out-of-body experience and one who professed to see spiritual beings) were so reluctant to share their experiences more widely. It wouldn't enhance their professional careers in a field where most look askance at such claims.

While these are my reflections, I feel confident that each reader who seeks evidence with an open mind, whether via their own experiences or those of others, will come to the same conclusion as I did: the evidence is compelling and overwhelming that God is real.

Precognitive Dreams

We often dream about people from whom we receive a letter by the next post. I have ascertained on several occasions that at the moment when the dream occurred the letter was already lying in the post-office of the addressee.
— C.G. Jung, *Synchronicity: An Acausal Connecting Principle*

It is foolish to be convinced without evidence, but it is equally foolish to refuse to be convinced by real evidence.
— Upton Sinclair, *Mental Radio*

The sensing of future events while in a dream state is a surprisingly commonplace phenomenon. One study of 234 Australian psychology students found 35 percent of the participants reported precognition in the form of dreams (and another 38 percent in the form of premonitions while wake).[15] Among the U.S. general population, surveys have indicated up to 50 percent of respondents experienced at least one recent, precognitive dream.[16] Whether known as precognitive dreams, prophetic dreams, or future sight, this acquiring of information about what looms, using means beyond presently available, traditionally attained, sense-based information, can be compelling evidence of the existence of a spiritual dimension and/or God.

The "precognitive" component of the term precognitive dreams is a difficult concept to accept and even harder to prove. Various scientific theories have sprung up to try and account for such. These explanations include selective memory bias (remembering the hits or accurate predictions and forgetting the misses), unconscious perception (unconsciously inferring future events from data), self-fulfilling prophecy (bringing the events to pass), and distorted memories (retrospectively fitting dreams onto subsequent events).

A scientific study of such phenomenon certainly offers challenges. Dreams are not exactly variables that can be controlled and replicated. But this doesn't mean that precognition in general lacks critically accepted scientific evidence. One notable example was published in 2011 in the prestigious *Journal of Personality and Social Psychology* by Daryl Bern (Department of Psychology, Cornell University).[17] Professor Bern conducted nine experiments designed to test two variants of psi: precognition (conscious perception of future events) and premonition (unconscious sensing or apprehension of the future). His experiments involved over one thousand subjects (Cornell University students). All but one of the experiments yielded results that were statistically significant: when the future event involved something emotion-laden (such as erotic images or negative stimuli), the students, on average, could foresee the event at a greater probability than chance.

Radin also reported evidence of precognition when the future event involved something of a highly arousing negative or erotic image,[18] and Bierman and Scholte found, in an MRI experiment monitoring brain activity, that a presentiment effect was demonstrated when the future event was arousing stimuli (in this case, bursts of noise).[19]

A meta-analysis of precognition also has been conducted, involving scholarly research articles by sixty-two different investigators conducting 309 experiments with more than fifty thousand subjects. The meta-analysis showed a small but significant hit rate on forced-choice precognition experiments—strong enough that the authors claimed the results unlikely to have been significantly inflated by the "file-drawer effect" (selective reporting of positive results).[20]

In terms of dream studies, notable experiments were carried out at Maimonides Medical Center in Brooklyn, New York.[21] While one subject slept in a room, being monitored with EEG leads, another person attempted to send images to the sleeper, who was then woken upon entering REM sleep. It was found, by independent judges blind to the procedures and purposes of the study, that there was a high correlation between dream images and those sent by the sender.

Of course, evidence of precognitive dreams—ones that give the dreamer insights into future events—is notoriously difficult to tackle in a controlled laboratory setting. How does one control what one dreams? Aren't precognitive dreams a very rare phenomena? Thus, the evidence is mainly in the form of anecdotal reports and surveys, both with notable shortcomings in terms of reliability and validity. Furthermore, if one holds the belief that life is not predetermined, then precognitive dreams can only predict what might occur; personal choice can impact the unfolding of what happens.

When it comes to precognitive dreams, let's be clear: unless you've had a particularly profound experience yourself, it's easy to dismiss the phenomena. When things don't fit into the scientific paradigm that colors your world, you either look for a new paradigm that includes the data, or you simply ignore the facts that don't fit. And ignoring is the effortless route.

In my own life, I rarely wake up with a strong sense of my previous night's dreams being anything more than chaotic events. There will be the usual anxiety-based dreams: the taking of a test without being prepared or of taking it in your underwear. Walking all over a parking lot or city blocks looking for your car. Being chased by little munchkins. There will be some repetitive dreams. One that I had repeatedly while an undergraduate was being chased by a ferocious black bear night after night, including its climbing up a tree after me. It was pretty terrorizing. At one point, I did learn a method to gain some measure of control over my dream state: Realizing that I indeed was dreaming, in those cases of self-awareness I could chase that bear without fear. I also could fly exhilaratingly above the treetops.

But precognitive dreams? I've had but two. But these two were remarkable and to an uncanny degree foretold forthcoming events. One dream was so strong and vivid that I awoke absolutely convinced that it revealed the future, and indeed it did to a stunning degree. This I call the "Savannah dream." Another equally unforgettable dream likewise proved to be a startling prediction of a very improbable event. This I call the "Pierangelo dream." Neither of these dreams could be adequately dismissed by any of the scientific speculations noted in the second paragraph above. To me, both provide persuasive evidence of spiritual phenomena.

Let's start with the PierAngelo dream.

PierAngelo dream

In April 1986, I was living in New York City, working for an international NGO. The graphic designer who fashioned our printed materials and conference banners was PierAngelo Beltrami.

PierAngelo, a graduate of a world-renowned graphic design and visual communications school in Italy, had been living in the New York City area during much of our organization's collaboration with him. However, in 1986 he was living and working in the Washington, D.C. area; I hadn't seen him, nor communicated with him, for a number of months. And, since we were no longer in active collaboration on projects, and since these were the days before the commercialization of the Internet and social media communications, I had pretty much lost contact with him.

Which made it all the more surprising when I had a vivid dream of PierAngelo racing a bicycle in the Olympics. He was one of three riders well ahead the pack as they approached the finish line. I was anxious to see if he would win, but the crowd rose up in excitement in front of me, obscuring my vision of the eventual winner. And then, I awoke.

What was equally surprising was to spot, the very morning after my dream, PierAngelo entering the lobby elevator in my office building on Fifth Avenue in downtown Manhattan. I joined him on the elevator and found that he had traveled up from Washington, DC that day for business with another company in the building, a media company occupying a different floor. The coincidence was so striking—the dream and his being in the building and very elevator with me—that I relayed to him my previous night's dream as we rode up in the elevator.

I still remember PA, as he was known to his friends, laughing heartedly upon hearing my recountal and then saying that my dream was quite impossible. He briefly hiked up his right pant leg, revealing that he didn't even have two full legs: his right limb was an artificial limb. As a 19-year old youth back in 1969, he had been in an accident on a motorcycle and had lost his leg below the knee after a botched operation had resulted in gangrene and amputation. So not only was he a little too old to be racing a bicycle in the Olympics, and never rode competitively, but he wore a prosthesis as well. I was somewhat startled by this revealing, but PA took it all in his characteristic good humor.

I didn't see PA the rest of the day, nor, to my recollection, for a long time afterward. By the time I chanced upon PA again in 1988, I had buried the memory about this absurd dream and the chance encounter in the elevator. I was sitting at a table at an event, eating a meal, when he approached me. His enthusiasm at seeing me was disarming until I heard what he had to say. "Rick, do you remember the dream you told me about in the elevator," he said. "Well, it came true. I'm going to compete in the 1988 Olympics in Seoul, Korea."

PA relayed that shortly after meeting me in Manhattan, a series of events took place that culminated in a most unusual situation: He was now a member of the U.S. cycling team scheduled to complete in South Korea—in a division of the Olympics known as the Paralympics. Scheduled immediately following the Olympic Games in the host country, Paralympic Games draw top athletes from around the world who have a physical disability. PA was in training with the U.S. Disabled Cycling Team to compete in this prestigious event.

How did this come about? A convergence of serendipitous events, beginning with his mother sending him an unexpected gift: a custom-made riding bicycle. Then, cycling around Washington, D.C. simply for exercise and enjoyment, PA chanced upon an advertisement for Paralympic trials for bike racing. This was followed by the good fortune of meeting a competitive cyclist who encouraged and advised him, and his surprising (to him) success in the cycling trials held for selecting members of the U.S. team. And now he was part of that national team, preparing in a training program in Colorado for the Paralympics.

PA's description of the eventual Olympic race sounded as it unfolded in the dream. With the crowd rising at the finish line, PierAngelo Beltrami maneuvered his single-pedal bike to a third-place finish in the fifty-five kilometer race, winning a bronze medal. It was his first international bicycle race. He found himself on the medal podium despite being, at nearly forty years old, almost twice the age of other competitors. He was the only U.S. cyclist to win a medal.

PierAngelo would go to win a silver medal in the ninth Paralympics held in Barcelona, Spain in 1992, as well as take a first place (1992) and second place (1991) in national races. In the four-kilometer race at the 1992 Paralympics, PA set a national record (6 minutes, 11 seconds). He set a world record during the time trials in the 200-meter race (14.294 seconds).

These competitions were not without their own curious stories. In his silver medal race at the ninth Paralympics, PA reported that, about a kilometer from the finish line, he had sensed a voice say "Go, now, go." This was right before a steep hill and, as he pushed like crazy in response to the voice, a way opened up that allowed him to get through the crowd of competitors and finish second. The other riders in that event were in their late twenties and early thirties; PierAngelo was forty-two years old and a grandpa. In another competition, he had little chance of finishing among the leaders until one of the riders made a mistake and caused a pileup of toppled riders and bikes, which he could avoid.

The initial dream was not a vague and mundane dream that could be interpreted in many ways: it was a specific dream involving a particular person (PierAngelo Beltrami) having success in a distinct event (a cycling completion) at the Olympics (albeit the division known as the Paralympics). The dreamer had no idea whether PierAngelo even rode a bicycle. The dream was followed by a rather remarkable set of "coincidences," including running into PA the very next morning in an elevator, after having not seen him in months, and PA receiving a custom-made bike as a birthday gift.

Clearly, PA had to make major effort to achieve Olympic victory and had the physical skills to accomplish such a feat; it turns out he was a gifted cyclist, with rare talent. But it was a talent which he was unaware of at the age of 36, when most cyclists are past their prime. PA had only begun riding a bicycle for recreation in 1985, a year before my dream. Even a seasoned skeptic must give pause in considering the odds associated with having such an improbable yet vivid dream come true, along with the other remarkable unfoldings—A dream and consequent developments that culminated in PierAngelo Beltrami being among the first three winners in this worldwide competition, the Paralympics in Seoul, Korea.

Savannah dream

Four years before the "PierAngelo dream" came the "Savannah dream."

In 1982, I was volunteering in Norfolk, Virginia for a project known as "Ocean Challenge," which was involved in marine educational and fishing activities. Sponsored by a nonprofit organization known as "Ocean Church," this program had as one of its goals—in addition to teaching navigation, seamanship, and fishing—to help people come closer to God via the natural environment. Of course, for many people, the encounter with the ocean was one of hanging over the side of the up-and-down, up-and-down, up-and-down, ever-jostling boat. Seasickness was a big drawback. One colleague described his seasickness this way: "I would alternate between thinking I was dying, thinking I was dead, and wishing I was dead."

But, as a biologist, it was a wonderful experience for me learning to fish with nets and navigation in general; I would spend hours learning about nautical terminology and reading books about boating. I loved the opportunity to interact with the marine fauna and see what each catch would bring. It was exciting to gain practical information about the ocean and sustainable development, and gain a vision of the potential the sea offered to feed the world's hungry.

When this nonprofit's national office decided to pioneer branch operations in several American cities, I was delighted for the opportunity to apply. I let it be known that I'd be pleased to go to whatever city the leadership felt was best for me.

One morning, as I roamed the home office where the Norfolk branch was headquartered, I chanced upon an open notebook that recorded the as-yet-unrevealed list of cities to which individuals were being assigned. It was an extensive list, but my name jumped out. I was assigned to Fort Pierce, Florida. I was quite at peace with that decision.

However, that same night I had a very vivid dream in which I found myself assigned to go to Savannah, Georgia. The dream even included seeing a map of the river system, and then myself on a boat on that river. I'd never been to Savannah; I was aware of the locale in the dream only because it was disclosed in the dream. The next morning I awoke with an absolute conviction that I was going to be appointed to Savannah.

However, as I reflected on the dream over the next few days, there was one discordant detail that bothered me. Not being familiar with Georgia, I had a preconception that Savannah was inland, not a very reasonable site to send a representative dealing with the ocean! And even in my dream Savannah was located on a river, not the ocean. Intrigued, I consulted an encyclopedia's entry for Savannah. (These were the days of physical, multi-volume encyclopedias; not scanning the Internet.) I found that not only was Savannah indeed on a river—one which connected this port with the ocean—but also I was struck by the similarity between the encyclopedia's map of the Savannah area and the river layout I'd seen in my dream.

However, I was skeptical of what might transpire should I share this dream. If I told anyone my dream, it possibly might travel up the chain of command to someone in authority, who would think: "What the heck. Let's send him to Savannah. He'll think it's God's Will, and it would inspire him." Then, if after sharing my dream I were to end up in Savannah, I'd never know for sure whether the dream was one of spiritual significance or whether more mundane reasons brought about my assignment to Savannah. So I kept the dream to myself; I didn't share it with anyone, not even my closest friends.

Two weeks passed as I waited for my assignment. My initial conviction that I was to go to Savannah faltered as time went on, blunted both because I already saw that I was assigned to go to Fort Pierce and the fact that I doubted Savannah as a possible site anyway. Nonetheless, I kept absolutely silent about my dream.

Then one day, an official from the headquarters office came to meet with me. As we sat at a small table adjacent to the living room, he informed me that the organization had originally slated me to go to Fort Pierce, Florida. However, he continued, "Something has come up. We had planned to send someone to Savannah, Georgia but that person cannot go there. It is an important future site for us. Rather than Fort Pierce, we would prefer if you would go instead to Savannah. Would you be willing to pioneer there, instead?" I sat there speechless as the person talked, getting that "twilight-zone"-type feeling.

To make a long story short, I did indeed go to Savannah. I pioneered the city alone. One of the stunning "coincidences" that occurred after my arrival are chronicled in a subsequent section.

Personal Experiences with the Spiritual Senses

*Alice laughed. 'There's no use trying," she said. "One can't believe impossible things."
"I daresay you haven't had much practice," said the Queen. "When I was your age, I always did it for half-an-hour a day. Why, sometimes I've believed as many as six impossible things before breakfast!"*
— Lewis Carroll, *Through the Looking Glass*

"I'm not afraid of death because I don't believe in it. It's just getting out of one car, and into another."
— John Lennon

Spirit, like God, denotes an object of psychic experience which cannot be proved to exist in the external world and cannot be understood rationally. This is its meaning if we use the word "spirit" in its best sense.
— Carl Jung, *Spirit and Life*

Human beings possess remarkable faculties for detecting and processing stimuli from their environment. The sense of sight allows us to detect electromagnetic energy within the visible range, opening up an amazing world of colors and shapes and movements. Likewise, changes in atmospheric particles, pressure, and different chemicals are detected by the senses of hearing, touch, taste, and smell. And these are just the five commonly discussed senses as first classified by Aristotle; today, authorities recognize at least nine different senses in humans and some classifications recognize as many as twenty-one senses. There is the sense of heat and absence of heat (thermoreception), and the perceptions of pain (nociception), balance (equilibrioception), and body awareness (proprioception).

However, throughout human history there also have been published reports of individuals experiencing another category of senses. The capabilities mentioned in the paragraph above are all physiological methods of perception, involving reception of stimuli by sensory cells. The sensory cells respond to a particular type of physical energy, which travels as nerve impulses to the brain, where the signals are analyzed. But many human beings report faculties involving the receiving and processing of stimuli of an incorporeal nature. For example, sacred scripture, popular books, and other media reference people who claim to see, hear, or even touch relatives or others who have passed away.

"Spiritual senses" is the designation for incorporeal methods of perception. Such faculties may be attributed to humans each having a soul or spirit, a concept that commonly is discussed in tandem with the existence of a "spiritual world" or afterlife. The associated spiritual senses allow recognition of such essences in other individuals or receiving stimuli originating in an incorporeal realm. (And certain experiences ascribed as involving the incorporeal may yet be attributed to physical attributes that humans have that we have not yet uncovered.)

Understandably, research into such a phenomenon is challenging because it is not easily amenable to the logical-scientific method of inquiry, involving objective, verifiable observation; rather, it involves personal, subjective experience. To be fair, many research methods still can be employed to investigate the phenomena, such as surveys, interviews, historical research, correlational studies, participant and nonparticipant observation, and meta-analysis. But the use of the most rigorous and trusted method of tackling cause and effect, various experimental methods involving control and test subjects, is not available, for these are non-controllable, subjective experiences, and ones that cannot be verified by an independent observer beyond the testimony of the experiencer. Nonetheless, the cataloging of such incidents adds support to the reality of spiritual senses and God.

The reported experiences with such senses are so ubiquitous, in all cultures and throughout recorded history, that it is not necessary to further point out examples. All readers are familiar with such reported phenomena. But I would like to add my own experiences to the literature, well aware of Richard Dawkins' admonition in *The God Delusion*, "If you've had such an experience, you may well find yourself believing firmly that it was real. But don't expect the rest of us to take your word for it."

The Nevada experience

The summer of 1978 saw the birth of the world's first test tube baby, the launching of the syndicated comic strip *Garfield*, and Argentina winning the FIFA World Cup. But for me, the summer is memorable for a life-transforming experience with the wonder of the spiritual senses.

The day began in a small town in Nevada. I was selling boxes of cookies door to door. While this had the practical function of raising funds for a nonprofit, for me it was all part of my then months-long spiritual quest to find out whether God existed, involving leaving my comfort zone. My reserved personality was ill suited to doing sales; not believing in God made the effort of door-to-door fundraising for charity all the more challenging.

I remember the day being hot and sunny as I visited a residential neighborhood of single-family, ranch-style homes. But mostly I remember suffering through a very difficult day, where I was being rejected house after house. Uncharacteristically—particularly for a small, remote town, where I typically have found people to have a friendly and generous spirit—everyone I encountered was being pointedly unfriendly to me. In some cases, I would barely begin letting the homeowners know what I was doing before I was being brusquely told, even yelled at, to leave.

And to make things worse, I noticed my voice getting progressively hoarse, seemingly from a quickly developing cold. I had no other symptoms: no cough, no dry or sore throat, no difficulty breathing or swallowing. But I certainly was losing my voice, and rapidly. I plodded on, but eventually my sentences were limited to only a few audible words. The rest were broken up by the apparent severe laryngitis. Finally, there was no point in continuing: my voice had become mostly incoherent.

I had visited that town with a fellow volunteer named Howard, who was also selling cookies. Returning to our car, I was delighted to find Howard back as well. At least I had someone with whom to commiserate. But Howard had returned because he needed more boxes of cookies: he was having great success. His obviously upbeat mood contrasted with my bleak outlook. As best I could with my disjointed voice, I relayed some of my day, apologizing that he couldn't understand me well with my voice so incoherent.

Howard seemed perplexed. "What are you talking about?" he queried. "Your voice sounds perfectly normal. There's no hoarseness. There's no breaking up of words or sentences."

If Howard was baffled, I was even more astonished by his comment. How could he not hear how disjointed and hoarse my voice was? We stood outside the car, pondering this for some time. I kept repeating, in a voice that couldn't enunciate half the syllables, how hoarse I was, while Howard reiterated that I was speaking normally.

It was then that I had a glimmer that maybe my sensory perception was not purely a physical experience: Was it possible that only I was hearing the hoarseness in my voice? Was this some type of spiritual or religious phenomenon?

Captivated by such an extraordinary possibility, and lost in the moment, I was astounded to suddenly note a change in my speaking with Howard: my voice now sounded magically whole and beautiful, even melodious. I'd never heard my voice with such a lyrical quality. Stunned by this change of events, I took my leave of Howard and, somewhat dazed and yet enthusiastic, headed out to the same neighborhood to continue my sales.

Now as I spoke with the people, I was enchanted by the metamorphosis in the sound of my voice, which seemed to modulate in pitch and tone like a beautiful song. Concomitantly, enraptured by the thought that this could be a spiritual experience, I was no longer centered on my woes, but my focus became one of cheerfully giving to others. The transformation in the neighborhood (read: me) was staggering. Sales were brisk. Almost everyone in the area purchased some boxes of cookies. People without exception were friendly and warm; some even approached me before I addressed them.

This auditory-vocal experience lasted for almost three months.

It was a very trying three months.

With time, I began to discern a pattern. It seemed that whenever I focused on myself—my goals, my appearance, my situation, the impression I was making on those listening—then my voice sounded to me as if it was very hoarse and disjointed. Sometimes it was so disjointed that I had difficulty speaking at all; it was that distracting. And the response from those being addressed in such a state was generally unfavorable. However, when I lost myself in the thought of giving to others, my voice resonated like a melody, very pleasant and agreeable. And people's response to me was invariably much better.

The perceived change in my voice could occur in the time it took for a thought. Once, as I was standing in front of an audience reading passages from a book, I was enjoying the lyrical quality of my voice and the rapt audience when I suddenly became concerned: What if my hoarse voice comes back? As soon as that thought bubbled up, my disjointed voice returned, and I could barely finish my reading because of the distracting aspect of the broken voice. I found that worrying about whether my voice would be hoarse was a sure inducer of the problem.

As promising an experience as this offered in terms of both understanding spiritual senses and training myself to think of others, I found myself increasingly self-conscious and exasperated by the phenomena. I began hoping beyond hope for the ever-present annoyance to be over, even turning to prayer in my desperation. When the phenomena at last dissipated, it was to my great relief.

With the retrospection of many years, I have learned to appreciate this phenomenon as a pivotal point in life. For it helped me to learn, when dealing with people, whether teaching a class or in one-on-one interactions, to turn my focus from myself, and how I am perceived, to how to give to others. For many this may come naturally; for me, this experience was a life-changing, wake-up moment. And one often at the forefront of my mind in interactions with others.

Meditation and the "peak experience"

Good luck, bad luck, fortune, "the breaks," "luck of the draw": These are terms that help capture the vicissitudes of life. One person, waiting in line to buy a lottery ticket, momentarily decides to buy a candy bar and is surprised when someone cuts in front of him in line; the person who lost his spot for a candy bar ends up winning the 319-million-dollar jackpot for himself and his six co-workers. Another person that same day decides to pass on the office pool and is not part of that winning jackpot.

For some, luck can be tied to faith or providence, with good luck sometimes viewed as a "blessing." Others may correlate good luck/bad luck with various superstitions (knocking on wood, Friday the 13th, black cat crossing in front of you, saying rabbit to usher in a new month, lucky numbers, seeing a raven, stepping on a crack, wearing your lucky underwear). For yet others, luck is purely random chance. In the ancient Roman religion, the goddess Bona Fortuna (good fortune) and the deity Bonus Eventus (good outcome or success) personified the concept of good luck.

In karmic belief, one's present-day experiences of seemingly good luck or bad luck are rooted in past acts and thoughts. And for many, the past linked acts and thoughts may extend back generations, with ancestral merit or demerit influencing their descendants' fortune. Many sacred texts advance such a view, for example passages in *Exodus* ("visiting the iniquity of the father upon the children to the third and fourth generation"); the Hindu *Laws of Manu* ("if the punishment falls not on the offender himself, it falls on his sons; if not on the sons, at least to his grandsons"), and the Taoist *Treatise on Response and Retribution* ("if any guilt remains unpunished at death, the judgement extends to the individual's posterity").

Whatever the cause, random chance or something more, a series of unforeseen events occurred during my second year in graduate school at Pennsylvania State University that proved life-altering.

These events were precipitated by a very sad time for my family, the passing of my beloved great-grandmother, Nellie Andrews. This pioneering woman had been an inspiration to all who knew her. With her husband, Fred, she established in 1912 the Old Homestead Restaurant in Daleville, Pennsylvania, and two years later the first gas pump in the area, as cars began to replace the horse and buggy. The Old Homestead Restaurant, whose patrons came from as far away as Philadelphia and New York City, also boasted the first telephone in the area and once served U.S. President Teddy Roosevelt on a political trip (related to a coal-mine strike) that he'd made to nearby Scranton. (The latter "good fortune" for my relatives was tied to a misfortune for the former president: his car had a flat tire right in front of the Old Homestead.)

After my great-grandmother's passing on October 20, 1976, I was surprised to receive a modest sum of money from her will. As I reflected on how to spend this money, I repeatedly begin to notice advertisements on the Penn State campus for an introductory lecture on transcendental meditation (TM). One of the most widely practiced forms of meditation, based on repetition of a mantra, TM was introduced by Maharishi Mahesh Yogi (1914-2008) and was tied to Hindu and Buddhist teachings.

Perhaps the ads for TM had been on the Penn State campus unnoticed by me for many days or months; I don't know. However, after the recurring sightings of the ads, I decided to attend an introductory lecture, to see whether such a course would be a good use of the money received. Specifically, I had a fervent question for which I was seeking an answer. I sat through the lecture until the end, when I could approach the speaker privately and inquire whether TM provided any insight in the matter. When my query was answered in the affirmative, I decided to sign up for the training.

My personal quest was to understand how to replicate and extend the "peak experience" that I would sporadically taste. This is a state of heightened awareness, confidence, creativity, and calmness. Since my high school days, but particularly during my undergraduate days at Bucknell University, I was captivated by the fortuitous appearance of this remarkable phenomenon, whereby I would undergo an intense increase in my focus, reasoning ability, and capacity to observe and remember details.

The coming of this special state was often as dramatic as it was unpredictable. I might be studying, taking an examination, writing, or jogging when it would seem as if there was a rushing sound in my ears, and I would be in this altered state of well-being. Whereas normally I was often shy and nervous in public settings, when the peak experience arrived I found that I could speak confidently to any audience. I also sensed having a great awareness of everything that was going on about me, such that I couldn't be surprised or startled; at the same time, I could focus remarkably on whatever I put my attention. I was never more at peace nor productive as when in this state.

For years I had been fascinated by this phenomenon, but its appearance and dissipation were unpredictable and uncontrollable. It happened rarely, and I found it impossible to induce or extend. The best correlate seemed to be via jogging (perhaps reflective of athletes finding themselves "in the zone"), but it was still rare and unpredictable and exhaustion accompanied that method. Surely, I reasoned, there must be some way to consistently enter this altered stated and without the downside of physical exertion. Was meditation a way?

The TM lecturer assured me it was. I decided it was worth probing.

From my very early efforts at meditation, I had experiences that were previously inconceivable. During a group meditation session during orientation, taken in a college classroom, I listened to the ticks of the wall clock progressively slowing down until there were large gaps between the ticks. I heard the word "flower" in my head and found it so uproariously funny, and was so bursting with joy, that I could barely contain my laughter. In subsequent sessions, I began to notice a lot of voices when I meditated: women's voices, men's voices, children's voices. At times, the repetition of the mantra would go on its own, effortlessly, as if I was just a bystander listening.

For the scientist in me, these were incomprehensible phenomena, but I subsumed them all under broad category: "subconscious." However vague the term, the labeling allowed me to move on, and I employed it many times. Subsequent experiences, such as the one described in the next section, led me years later to wonder whether "spiritual phenomena" or "spiritual senses" might be more apt terminology.

Early in my training in meditation, I did obtain my goal of achieving the peak experience. I entered into this desirable state for three days in a row—a startling departure from the one-day maximum I had experienced previously. Until then, the state would disappear overnight as I slept. But for three days, I was enveloped in an extraordinary state of peace, focus, calm, and well-being.

Another longer-term result ensued: I became much more aware of things, as if my mind had cleared from a robotic, conditioned existence. This manifested in multiple ways. I was seeing signage and other environmental features I'd never noticed. I was more observant of others and sensitive to the impacts of my words and actions on them; I notably became more giving in my behavior. It even impacted my driving pattern. I had been driving the same route every day to and from the university, as if part of my autonomic nervous system, below the level of consciousness. Now, I explored many alternative routes, learning the different light patterns, and finding better routes for different days and times of the day.

Overall, the meditation proved to be life transforming and ultimately would be a key contributor to my interest in spiritual phenomenon, laying groundwork for me to accept years later the reality of spiritual senses and God. However, I also ended up having one terrible experience with meditation, an odd and scary episode that ultimately led to my discontinuing this practice. This I detail next.

Mediation possession

After a few months of practicing meditation, mostly with enjoyable and rewarding sensations, I began to have a most distressing response every time I would meditate. As I would sit on a chair upright and repeat my mantra, I found my mood transforming from ordinary to one whereby I was consumed with anger and resentment. I also felt as if my head was being pulled backwards. Over time, the emotions became so overwhelming, and the tugging so agonizing, that I went to the local meditation center for some guidance. When I described my troubling experience, I received rather strong guidance: "Do *not* fight this during meditation and definitely do *not* stop a meditation session when experiencing this. Just finish the meditation. If it doesn't go away after a while, please come back and see us."

But the distressing meditations continued, session after session, day after day after day. The anger enveloping me was as strong as ever, and I dreaded both it and the neck stain I felt from my head being drawn backwards.

Then one day I reached my limit. In the midst of a meditation filled with intense wrath, with my head being wrenched backwards, I exclaimed "enough is enough," and I yanked my head forward, stopping the session right then and there.

Instantly, it was as if I were a different person. No longer meditating, I was now openly filled with rage. Whereas previously the intense emotions would disappear when I ceased meditating, now they remained with me. My normal state didn't return.

I went to the laboratory/office space that I shared with two other graduate students in the Biology Department, but I couldn't keep my emotions in check. When another graduate student, Pete, an invariably pleasant and unassuming individual, arrived and politely volunteered to check my mailbox for me, I inexplicably yelled at him, for no reason and in the harshest of terms. Pete didn't say a word, just looked at me as if wondering "what just happened here?" I found myself struggling to get control of my emotions. I felt as if I was a little person inside my mind telling myself: "What are you doing? What is going on?" Finally, I gathered myself for a minute and started to apologize: "I am sorry, Pete. I don't know—" Instantly, I launched into another outburst of uncontrollable hatred. Worse yet, as a person who didn't swear, my vocabulary was filled with swear words.

Shortly thereafter, another graduate student, Doug, entered and my rage-filled eruption continued. Pete and Doug both looked at me perplexed. My behavior was so out of character that neither responded. I myself couldn't understand at all what had overcome me, and why I could not seem to get myself under control. Finally, I was able to walk away and go into an empty classroom. There, for over one hour my fury continued. I was like a madman: throwing chalk, pushing chairs around, ranting—all the while trying to get control of my emotions and feeling like an alien inside my own body.

After some time, I returned to my apartment, sat down, and pushed myself to mediate once again. While my resentment and anger persisted, it was somewhat controlled during this twenty-minute session. Remarkably, when I finished mediating, I was surprised to find that the anger had complete dissipated. I had returned to my normal state.

I was stunned by what had transpired. I returned embarrassed to the laboratory and apologized to Pete and Doug. I recall Pete remarking that my actions hadn't bothered him because they were so uncharacteristic of me that he'd understood something was going on.

Within a few days, I returned to the meditation center to report my experience and was even more strongly admonished never to suddenly stop my mediation in the midst of such emotions. However, unnerved by the experience and alarmed by what I had unleashed inside myself, coupled with the continually painful mediations, I soon discontinued meditating entirely.

This rapid transformation in my personality and the sudden reversal, something that I'd never before or since experienced, remains perplexing to this day. A psychologist may be able to categorize the experience; a religious scholar may label it spirit possession; a pragmatist may question why it even matters since it was a one-off that has never recurred. But it was such a powerful and unusual experience, and one that does find correlation with reports of spirit possession—the hearing of voices; the irrational anger without a trigger; the feeling of separation from one's own body; the uncharacteristic and uncontrollable actions while in the state; the abrupt and absolute dissipation of the phenomenon, also without a trigger—that I add this experience to the literature in the field.

Hearing a voice

Many people report auditory spiritual experiences, such as hearing voices of long-dead relatives. I have encountered many first-person testimonies of such phenomena, among a host of reported visual, olfactory, and tactile accounts. Perhaps even the well-known curiosity of synesthesia, where there is a mixing of senses, may involve some dimension of spiritual senses. In synesthesia, a person may "hear colors," or "see sounds." For example, composer Franz Liszt claimed to see colors when hearing musical notes. (Some individuals see colors assigned to particular letters, numbers, or days of the week. Nobel Laureate physicist Richard Feynman claimed such for physics equations: "When I see equations, I see the letters in colors—I don't know why.")

I myself blissfully have gone most of my life without such experiences, with the exception of the cacophony of voices heard during meditation. However, in October of 1977 I had a brief but powerful encounter with an unexplained voice.

Attentively immersed in a lecture on the life of a religious leader, I was suddenly overcome by an attack of drowsiness. Valiantly fighting off this sleepiness, suddenly I heard a very clear and loud man's voice, as if filling the room. The booming words were perplexing and their delivery sounded filled with anguish: "Oh, nooo! It's too late. It's too late." I quickly looked around at the faces of those near me, wondering what had just happened. Clearly, no one had heard the voice.

The sheer strength and power of those words, spoken in an unfamiliar voice, shook me greatly at the time and resonated with me for many days; this abnormal experience remains vivid yet today. But, in the aftermath of hearing the troubled voice, grasping vainly for a rational explanation, I vaguely attributed the experience to "hearing my subconscious" and left it at that.

Certainly, the mysteries of the mind are far from being understood. Yet, given the universality of reported spiritual experiences of many types, I am inclined to put greater weight on the possibility of this being an auditory spiritual experience versus an "unconscious or subconscious mind" that decides to cry out loudly and in someone else's voice. I add this first-person account to the data in the field.

Synchronicity

*Coincidence is the pseudonym dear God chooses
when he wants to remain incognito.*
— Albert Schweitzer

Coincidences are spiritual puns.
— G.K. Chesterton

Rule 39: There is no such thing as a coincidence.
— Leroy Jethro Gibbs, *NCIS*

Human life is replete with coincidences—the surprising concurrence of two or more events whose linkage appears both meaningful and lacking an obvious causal connection. One can take as an example someone thinking of a former schoolmate just before that schoolmate calls on the telephone or before chancing upon that schoolmate on a city street.

It's possible that most people experience meaningful or even extraordinary coincidences at least occasionally.[22] Thalbourne conducted a survey in which twenty-five percent of the respondents reported that they "often" experienced "truly astounding coincidences," and sixty-four percent reported such circumstances "now and then"; all reported at least one "truly astounding coincidence."[23]

Indeed, the literature is replete with some rather stunning examples. Take the case chronicled by Wilhelm Franz Johannes von Scholz in *Der Zufall und das Schicksal*. In 1914, a woman took a photograph of her son in the Black Forest. She dropped off the film in Strasbourg to be developed, but was unable to pick it due to the outbreak of war. Two years later, she bought a film in Frankfurt to take a picture of her daughter. When she had the film developed, it was double exposed—with the photo of her daughter superimposed on the lost photo of her son. Somehow, the original film hadn't been developed and instead ended up back in circulation among new films in another city, and she was the one to purchase it.[24]

Or take the curious case reported by McManus:

Every day weird things happen for which there are no rational explanations. Take, for example, the case of Retch Sweeney's watch. Retch and I were trolling on a lake in Canada several years ago and, as he leaned over the side of the boat to net a nice rainbow trout I was bringing in, Retch's watch came loose from his wrist and fell into the lake. Not only was the watch expensive, but it held great sentimental value....

Five years after Retch lost his watch in the Canadian lake, he and I went on a boat-camping trip on a lake in Montana. It is important to note that there is no waterway connecting the two lakes. After making camp, Retch and I went out to see if we couldn't hook into one of the monster rainbows reported in the vicinity. Sure enough, as we trolled past the mouth of a stream, Retch's rod whipped double and a few seconds later a beautiful rainbow was doing aerial gymnastics. We went back to camp and while I started preparing supper, Retch dressed out his fish. Suddenly he let out a great yell. I rushed over to see what had happened.

"Look what I found in this rainbow," he shouted, holding up a shiny object.

"I can scarcely believe my eyes," I said. "How could such a thing happen?"

"Beats me," Retch said. "I've never even heard of anybody finding a bottle cap in the stomach of a fish before."

"Me either," I said. "Now if it had been the watch you lost in the lake up in Canada, I could understand that. You read in the newspapers all the time about that sort of thing happening."

Ok, this last one is a classic misdirection from my favorite humorist Patrick F. McManus in *Never Sniff a Gift Fish*. I included this from the late McManus because it illustrates just how widely recognized the coincidence phenomena is that readers think they know where McManus is heading.

I have titled this chapter "synchronicity," utilizing the term Swiss psychologist Carl Jung coined to describe "a meaningful coincidence of two or more events where something other than the probability of chance is involved." In his work *Synchronicity: An Acausal Connecting Principle*, Jung provided many examples, including the Schloz example and the one quoted in a previous chapter: "We often dream about people from whom we receive a letter by the next post. I have ascertained on several occasions that at the moment when the dream occurred the letter was already lying in the post-office of the addressee."

Jung, considered the founder of analytical psychology, accumulated reports of meaningful coincidences and considered them not to be chance but rather the product of a universal consciousness. In fact, Jung engaged in gathering all kinds of data on phenomena that often are considered to fall outside of normal rational explanation.

I might have titled this chapter simply "coincidences." Mathematicians Persi Diaconis and Frederick Mosteller, in their paper "Methods for studying coincidences," define the term similar to Jung's synchronicity: "A coincidence is a surprising concurrence of events, perceived as meaningfully related, with no apparent causal connection." However, the term "coincidence" has become so commonly used in a dismissive manner to counter someone's attributing meaning to a linkage of events—"Ah, that's just a coincidence"—that the term impedes the openness desired. While Jung's nomenclature has its own shortcomings, it is a rare-enough term that at least it isn't immediately associated with dismissal of meaningful linkages as purely the product of chance.

This is not to say that there aren't valid reasons to have a healthy skepticism of reported coincidences. For one, humans do tend to be wired to seek meaningful patterns. And sometimes these perceived patterns are more creations of the mind than anything more. There is even a name for the inclination to see patterns in random data: apophenia. Thus, some coincidences may be explained as the brain simply noting a concurrence between two or more events or circumstances and attaching significance to those linkages.

And then there is the issue of the truly large numbers involved with human interactions. From a statistical perspective, the occurrence of coincidences in daily life is inevitable and often may be less remarkable than one might expect: after all, there are about eight billion people on the planet, engaging in countless activities each day. Put just twenty-three people in a room together and there is already a greater than 50 percent chance that two individuals will share the same birthday. For many people, coincidences are just that: statistically unremarkable events that occur just by chance or pure luck, lacking any meaningful or important connotations.

It is certainly likely that too many people tend to read far too much into spurious correlations—and tend to ignore all the times that such linkages do not occur. I mean how many times do you run to tell your family and friends about the time you were thinking of a particular person, someone you hadn't seen in years, and then, during that same day, you didn't run into the person? Cue the McManus tale above.

But confirmation bias works both ways, and the explanations above give the impression of ones designed to fit into a paradigm where events couldn't be meaningfully linked due to a divine power or spirit. Wouldn't dismissing remarkable linkages of events because of a preconceived bias that there is no higher power, just chance and a pattern-finding brain, be as much a misuse of critical thinking as arbitrarily ascribing a higher power to each meaningfully linked event? Statistical probabilities and a brain that creates meaning where none exists are not evidences but suggested explanations; the cataloging of remarkable linkages provides direct data. This chapter is designed to add to the data on reported meaningful coincidences.

Of course, one complication with narrating coincidences is "egocentricity bias": while people experiencing coincidences tend to see them as noteworthy and surprising, others hearing about the same experiences tend to be dismissive and attribute to them a high likelihood of having occurred by chance. Indeed, as I was drafting this very section on coincidences, I had an experience that impressed me, but barely drew a raised eyebrow from others. I asked my wife if she had called the plumber to get our furnace cleaned for the winter. She said she didn't have the number. Within ten minutes, I found the number, and as I held the slip of paper with the number in my hand, intending to call the plumber, the plumber called to set up an appointment for cleaning the furnace. Stunning to me—I couldn't even remember the last time the plumber had called me, if ever—but unimpressive to my wife and son listening nearby.

When ten years later, shortly after starting anew on this book, I had another surprising experience, I didn't even bother sharing with my family because I already knew it wouldn't raise an eyebrow. As I was shopping in the local grocery store, I began to think about someone that I hadn't thought of in years: the parent of a boy who'd played baseball with one of my sons. I imagined running into him in the store and then asking him about how his son was doing. The fanciful musing was remembered precisely because the parent was someone of whom I never thought. I left the store and who should I run into? Well, not him. Nobody, really. And that would have been it except when I got back home, I realized I'd forgotten to pick up something my wife had asked for. About an hour later I finally was able to return to the store and that was when I turned the corner of an aisle and was startled to run into this person. (This person immediately recognized me and greeted me warmly. Already having rehearsed a conversation with this person, and ever quick with the quip, I responded "Hi" and awkwardly continued on my way. For those who were wondering, "l'espirt de l'escalier" is the term for coming up with a clever retort or witty conversational piece a little too late. I don't know what the French term is for not coming up with any conversational piece at all.)

This is one of those encounters that probably no one finds surprising except myself. And yet, there are many quite stunning coincidences in the literature. And innumerable people experience either such striking coincidences in their lives, or so many small coincidences, that they see this as more than chance. Indeed, Thalbourne's survey revealed that more than half of his respondents (58 percent) agreed or strongly agreed with the statement that "I am quite sure that there might be a Divine Hand at work in what we call coincidence, whether immediately meaningful on the surface or not."

With the above precautions in mind, I offer below several personal experiences that I put in the category of "truly astounding and meaningful coincidences." They are but a sample of surprising alignments of events that I remember from my own life. Statistically unremarkable? Random events? Seeing a pattern where none exists? One cannot discount the possibility. Yet, I believe, in their totality, these remarkable events are suggestive of something more than happenstance and, indeed, hint at the likelihood of some other force at work.

Savannah, Georgia Two

Not long after the earlier recounted dream presaging a trip to Savannah, Georgia, I arrived in this port city by bus from Norfolk, Virginia. It was the fall of 1982.

Savannah is a beautiful southern city, with buildings both historic and architecturally fascinating, and many squares with fountains and monuments. There are historic churches, including Christ Church, where early rectors included the well-known John Wesley and George Whitefield. Savannah also is known for its hospitality and was once known as "Hostess City of the South."

The purpose of my being in Savannah was to pioneer Ocean Challenge in the city. Situated on the Savannah River, the diverse city of about one hundred and fifty thousand people is the largest port in the state of Georgia. My goal was to first develop a financial foundation and then establish both an educational and fishery operation.

I wanted to truly challenge myself. With missionary zeal, I arrived in Savannah with little money and no place to stay. I brought some fashion/costume jewelry to present door-to-door in order to raise money for a place to rent until I could find employment, ideally in a fishery related business. During the day, I would go from home to home and business to business offering this jewelry and collecting donations. (On one occasion, I had collected a lot of coins during the day. Returning home quite late at night, while most of the city slept, I ran into two men who asked me for money. I said I didn't have any, and then in one of the most inept efforts at providing supporting evidence, absent-mindedly hit my bulging, coin-filled pockets to show them how broke I was. Which caused a great clattering of coins, followed by me running down the empty streets of Savannah, pursued by two men intent on robbing me.)

Because of my lack of money, the first place that I stayed in Savannah was little more than a flophouse. I had stayed in similar quarters some six years earlier, when I decided to experience the life of a migrant worker in Washington State, with a brief stint also in a homeless shelter. However, my Savannah "residence" felt even less secure than those locations.

The building in which I stayed was several stories high. My room lacked a bed, but did have a mattress on the floor. The bathroom was a shared one. The door on my room lacked a lock—but I had few possessions to be concerned about. Nonetheless, it was more than a little disconcerting one night, while asleep, to have three men burst into the room and sit down on the mattress, not realizing the room had been rented out.

Which brings me to an unusual set of coincidences.

Early one Saturday evening, as I returned to the building from a day of raising funds, I was approached by a well-dressed, middle-aged couple standing outside. They informed me that they were looking into something that had happened to a young relative of theirs, a troubled boy who had fallen from a third-floor room of that building earlier in the week. He was now in the hospital in serious condition. They enquired if I knew "whether he had fallen by accident or had been pushed?" Although I didn't know anything about the situation, this couple wrote their name and address on a slip of paper in the hope that I might chance across information. I politely took the paper and put it into my shirt pocket.

The next day, on a recommendation from an acquaintance, I attended a Unitarian Universalist Church service in a downtown church building that was a landmark for its antiquity. Originally dedicated in 1851, the church building was popularly referred to as the "Jingle Bells Church." It had been the musical director of this church, James Pierpont (uncle of financier J. Pierpont Morgan), who had composed the famous winter song "One Horse Open Sleigh," which gained fame as "Jingle Bells." The song had been copyrighted in 1857.

The service was not as memorable as what happened near its conclusion. After the main program, there was a time for discussion and announcements. The very woman sitting next to me in the pew rose to address the congregation: "I've been doing social work with a troubled, young boy who recently fell, or was pushed, from the third floor of a downtown apartment building. I need to locate his relatives, but I haven't been able to. Would anyone here know how I could find them?" A highly unusual question to ask I thought, but, then again, I was sitting next to her with the relative's address in my pocket. I fumbled around until I found the slip of paper and gave her the address.

Airplane coincidences

First flight. My very first airline flight was also my first of several improbable "airline coincidences." It was the summer of 1979, and I was traveling on a jumbo jet from San Francisco to New York City. My goal was to attend an orientation for new students beginning a course of graduate study at an upstate interfaith seminary.

As I took my aisle seat, I became acutely aware that I was ill-prepared to get to the meeting site. I was unfamiliar with New York City. And in this age before the Internet, and having been immersed in my work until right before the trip, I was winging the excursion more than mapping out any plans. Nonetheless, I assumed that I could catch a taxi ride to the address that I had.

Part way into the flight, I took out a religious text, *The Divine Principle*, to read. Suddenly, I was slapped on my left shoulder. Stunned, I turned to look at the stranger seated directly across the aisle who had struck me. He explained that when he saw what I was reading he realized I was probably of the same faith. We soon discovered that we were headed to the same destination, the Unification Theological Seminary.[25]

This man, Mark, proved to be God-send. For, it turned out that the seminary was not in New York City, nor even in the suburbs. It was at a little town called Barrytown, over one hundred miles from New York City! My plans for a taxi ride would have proved fruitless (or extremely expensive). Instead, Mark had mapped out his plans and together we took a train to our destination.

Mark and I hadn't known each other before the trip, and I was unaware of anyone else in the San Francisco area traveling to this destination. We had booked our tickets independently. It was a large plane with many passengers. The incoming seminary class had only about forty students, coming from all over the country and from a number of nations. And yet, Mark and I had been positioned right across the aisle from one another.

Porto Murtinho. In 1998, I was working in the Pantanal. The world's largest freshwater wetland system, the Pantanal extends over millions of hectares of central-western Brazil, northeastern Paraguay, and eastern Bolivia. Just south of the Amazon Basin, and occupying one-third of the Upper Paraguay River Basin, this immense floodplain region (larger than many countries, including England and Austria, and twenty-nine of the U.S. states, including Florida and New York State) is one of the world's great natural wonders. Its extraordinarily concentrated and diverse flora and fauna makes it one of the world's great reservoirs of plant and animal life and an ecological paradise.

On May 11, 1998, I was traveling from New York City back to my work in the Pantanal on a Varig Airbus, with the first stop in São Paulo. I sat in window seat 18A, separated by an empty seat from a man in aisle seat 18C. This person's persistent effort to strike up a conversation with me was mostly met with indifference; this was a red-eye flight and my plan was to sleep and catch up on my reading.

Finally, just before dinner, as the trays of food were being served, this man turned to me and said: "You look familiar. Do I know you?" I assured him that I did not know him, but then politely asked him his final destination. He replied that he changed planes in São Paulo, en route to Campo Grande. Campo Grande is the capital and largest city in the interior state of Mato

Grosso do Sul, one thousand kilometers (over 600 miles) from São Paulo. This man further explained that once he arrived in Campo Grande, he would then proceed to a small city.

This person, Manuel, had now caught my attention. There were a lot of small cities and towns to which he could have been going. However, by 1998 I had had enough unusual experiences to intuit what Manuel would say next—that the small municipality to which he was going was Porto Murtinho.

For Porto Murtinho, which is some seven hours by land from Campo Grande and near the southern limit of the Pantanal, was where I was headed. Furthermore, he was coming to work on the project in which I was engaged.

Manuel had never been to Porto Murtinho and had made no advance plans as to how to get to the city. He had planned to travel with two other co-workers, but they had been delayed a day and so he kept his flight. In a sort of reverse scenario from my first airline flight, it was I who had planned ahead of time, having arranged for a driver from Porto Murtinho who was coming to Campo Grande to pick me up. I told Manuel that we would be able to travel together, to his great relief. Furthermore, the flight from São Paulo to Campo Grande makes a number of stops on the way. Manuel started to get off at the first, and wrong stop, during the flight. It was a mistake that his two later-arriving colleagues actually would make, finding themselves stranded in another town for hours. Manuel's being seated next to me on the Varig Airbus had been a God-send for him.

Manuel and I had used different travel agents. He had secured seat 18C at the airport counter just prior to the flight; I had used my travel agent to arrange my seat 18A. In response to my inquiry, the stewardess stated there were over 280 seats on the flight.

São Paulo Flight 2. A year later, I once again found myself traveling alone on a flight to São Paulo, this time on a 747. The flight was packed, and I found myself in a middle seat in the middle row of the economy section—the least preferred seat on an airplane. There seems to be some unwritten principle of territorial sovereignty that if you get this seat, then the "shared" armrests are the territory of those on your left and on your right, and with five seats across in this section, you have to ask two passengers to move should you want to get up on this nine-hour flight.

Directly in front of me was a young American couple who were loudly expressing their agitation with being squeezed in such middle seats on this red-eye flight. In particular, the woman was peeved and demanding that the stewardess fix this situation. But the stewardess, already dealing with a nearly full flight, could do little more than encourage the couple to find on their own passengers to switch seats with them.

After the plane gained cruising altitude, the American woman headed up the left aisle. She returned gleefully: she had found someone next to one of the rare empty seats who would switch seats with her. They quickly gathered their belongings and headed up to the next section to make the switch.

To my great surprise, the person who made the switch with them, and who would take the seat right in front of me, was Fatima. Fatima was a long-time acquaintance of my wife and me, and when we lived in Long Island for a couple of years, she even had a room in the house we were renting. However, I had lost contact with Fatima for a number of years and had no idea that she was on this flight. We immediately locked eyes in surprise.

Ironically, I had been thinking that I needed to track down Fatima. A native Brazilian, at the time working in the banking industry in New York, Fatima had many high-level contacts in her home country. I was working on an event in Brazil where I knew she would be helpful in contacting certain Brazilian VIPs.

With her seat directly in front of me, we were able to carry on an effective conversation on this issue.

There have been other airline coincidences that I have experienced, but these three share a common thread. These were flights on large airplanes in which I ended up seated next to someone "by chance" in which the encounter was unique and singularly important. At what point does a series of coincidences become a pattern?

Balch Hall, Cornell University

In the fall of 2009, one of my daughters was headed to Cornell University as part of the freshman class. As with most any parent in the modern era, my wife and I worried about our child in the college environment. During her high school years, she had exceptional friends—girls who would make any parent proud. New to the university and the area, isolated from friends and family, in a place with unique peer pressures, would our daughter find schoolmates of similar values? What would her dormitory life be like? My wife and I prayed that she would be able to connect to students of shared moral values.

On Friday, August 21, we drove our daughter to Cornell, about a two-hour drive from our home in northeastern Pennsylvania. Freshman at Cornell arrive about one week prior to the other students in order to have orientation. As we pulled onto the campus, we could see that there were quite a few freshman dormitories, ten or so, to accommodate the three thousand incoming freshman. Our daughter was assigned to a single room on the sixth floor of Balch Hall.

As my wife and I were helping our daughter to move in (hauling everything up six flights—no elevator to the sixth floor!), I received a phone call from an acquaintance who lives in Ithaca, where Cornell is situated. Ann Hoover and her husband Chad share the same religious tradition as my wife and I. Ann informed me that she was with another family of an incoming freshman who likewise belonged to the same faith, and she wanted to know whether we would like to meet the family. The thoughtful gesture was warmly embraced: My wife and I only knew of one other incoming freshman with the same, small-in-numbers faith tradition and that was a male student.

When we met the other family, I was surprised to find out that this new student was the granddaughter of the chairman of the board of the same organization where I was employed. The conversation then moved to which dorm the student had been assigned. Surprise again: she had just moved into Balch Hall. What floor, we inquired, wondering if our daughter might be close enough to share time with this person. Once again, my wife and I were astonished: This other student also was going to be on the sixth floor. Although the sixth floor encompassed a lot of rooms, it was possible, we surmised, that they would be part of the same wing of the building.

Somewhat later in the day, after attending some orientation functions, my wife, my daughter, and I returned to her new room in Balch Hall. As we reached the sixth floor landing, we found the other family on the same landing, not far from our daughter's room. After some confused "small world" conversation, I walked to our daughter's room, wondering where exactly this other coed was situated.

As we read the signs on the doors identifying each student's name, we were surprised to find out that this other student was situated in the room right next to our daughters.

Among the three thousand incoming students, housed in ten dorms, on many floors and many rooms, our daughter and this daughter of an associate, of the same faith tradition, had ended up next door neighbors. Neither family had been aware of the other and had made no special arrangements regarding room assignment. Yet, they ended up right next to each other, where together they could navigate the transition to college.

Borders

As noted above, one person's coincidence is another's mathematical probability. Thus, although people are often fascinated with coincidences that happen to them, they are often little more than interesting party stories for others.

Yet, the coincidences being recounted here are only a selection of meaningful coincidences, intimating a tableau of a world a lot more interesting than simple mathematical probability. Deepak Chopra in his book *Seven Spiritual Laws of Success*, Shakti Gawain in *Creative Visualization*, and Norman Vincent Peale in *Positive Imaging* all reference how a person's thoughts can mobilize the energy of the universe to attract corresponding experiences, events, and people, or as Chopra puts it, "activate the field of infinite correlation." It's similar to a tuning fork, resonating at a fixed tune, initiating vibrations in a nearby tuning fork of the same pitch.

I think all three authors would see the following as fitting that model.

This account revolves around a Border's bookstore, which was part of a chain of book and music retailers that once had stores around the world, but in 2011 went bankrupt and shut down. And it revolves around planning for an event that led to an unexpected synchronicity.

The date was Friday, January 14, 2011. That morning, my family drove in two vehicles to an event and catering facility in the historic Green Ridge section of Scranton, Pennsylvania. After completing preparations for an event planned for the next day, we headed out for what was to be a quick tour of the nearby Worthington campus of Pennsylvania State University. When the visit turned out much longer than expected, as my son and daughter-in-law spent time with someone from the admissions department, I advised my wife to head out with the rest of the family to go to a nearby restaurant and hold seats for us. I would wait with the second car for my son and daughter-in-law to complete their meeting, and then we would rendezvous at the restaurant.

I suggested the nearby Denny's, a few minutes' drive away. When the three of us finally departed the Worthington campus, I fully expected that was where we would be eating.

Here is where the story gets odd.

As my son, daughter-in-law, and I drove toward Denny's, I called my wife to let her know we were on our way. At the same time, my daughter-in-law called a friend in the area to touch base.

I am sure that my daughter-in-law's conversation with her friend, Eileen, went better than my conversation with my wife, Lourdes. In my dialogue, the answer to my inquiry "Are you at Denny's?" was not what I expected. I was literally flabbergasted to hear my wife tell me they had decided to go to a small café in a Borders bookstore: "What? That's far away. Why in the world would you go there? Do they even have much in the way of food there? I thought everyone was hungry?" Lourdes said that everyone was hungry, but had trouble deciding where to go, and for some reason they decided to go to the Borders café. My wife apologized, but my efforts to talk her into going to a real restaurant was met with the information that they'd already arrived at the Borders. I turned the car around and headed there.

Meanwhile, my daughter-in-law got off the phone with her friend. As I relayed that we were headed to Borders to eat, she expressed surprise, as that is where Eileen said she was at that moment. I didn't really know Eileen; this was a startling confluence of events to make the introduction.

Entering the Borders only increased the oddity. There at one small table sat Eileen, working on her computer. At the two tables right next to her, as oblivious to Eileen's presence as she was to theirs, was my family. I was immediately humbled for having been exasperated that this café had been chosen.

One might have a hard time calculating the mathematical probability of such an encounter. Scranton is not a small hamlet: it is Pennsylvania's sixth most populous city and the metro area has over five hundred thousand people. There are innumerable eating establishments between the PSU Campus and the mall area where Borders was located. And I would consider the Borders one of the least likely places for our family to gather for lunch. It was a bookstore; it was out-of-the-way; it had a tiny cafe area, with only a few chairs per each small table; it didn't offer the food selection for the substantial lunch planned. To all of this then add that the conversation between my daughter-in-law and Eileen, and between my wife and me, was simultaneous, uncoordinated. Yet, my family ended up at adjacent tables with Eileen. One can begin to visualize how Chopra's, Gawain's, and Peale's hypotheses about the energy of the universe attracting corresponding experiences, events, and people might offer an intriguing proposal.

Three in a photo

I experienced a perplexing phenomenon in 1979, during a three-week orientation/seminar for new students to the Unification Theological Seminary in Barrytown, New York (the orientation mentioned above under "First Flight"). I have included this account not because it offers convincing evidence of synchronicity, but rather for its life-transforming lesson.

For reasons unfathomable to me, I just could not stand two men at the orientation. These two individuals, Jim and

Barry, were about my age and seemed like pleasant-enough individuals. They were thoughtful and not given to displays of arrogance or self-centeredness that might normally induce negative reactions. I had little interaction with them, at least not in any memorable detail, so it wasn't anything they said or did to me. Yet, every time that I'd see them, I had a strong emotional reaction of revulsion.

During the orientation, I studiously tried to avoid Jim and Barry. I wouldn't sit at their tables in the cafeteria and avoided being part of any small-group discussions or breakout sessions of which they were part. I couldn't put my finger on what bothered me about them, and even at the time realized my feelings were irrational. It made no sense. But, such were my feelings.

Near the end of the three weeks, the time came to take pictures. It was decided that the pictures would be taken in groups of three. Of course, I hoped that I wouldn't have my photo taken with either of them. The odds were good. There were about forty people in the seminar and our last names were vastly different should the groupings be alphabetical.

Of course, what happened was the photo coordinator put exactly us three together. First Jim and Barry were singled out, and then, as I tried to make myself small, I was asked to be the third.

As the photographer got ready to snap the photo, he suddenly stopped and made a surprising observation: "Isn't that remarkable. You three look very much alike."

I hadn't realized this before, but yes, undeniably, we were very similar in physical appearance. Indeed, for years later individuals would often get our names confused, calling me Jim or Barry. Even when Barry was stationed overseas in Germany, I would occasionally meet people from Germany who would remark how much I reminded them of someone that they'd met in Germany. I would ask if it were Barry, and they would exclaim, "Why, yes!"

In a group of about forty, the odds of that particular group being selected randomly is small: about one hundreds of one percent. We were not part of any natural group during the seminar. Our last names were dissimilar. I was not standing near them when the decision was made for the three of us to be in the photograph. Yet, this placement had occurred.

And because it had happened, I was able to receive an important insight. I understood that Jim and Barry were not the source of my repulsion, for I didn't even know them. The source was within myself. It was as if I disliked something about myself and saw that somehow reflected in Jim and Barry.

Later, after the orientation, I went on to become good friends with both Jim and Barry, and I got to like them both very much, for there was a lot to admire in their characters. But I learned a profound lesson in that seminar that has forever colored my understanding of liking and disliking certain people. This insight arose because of the "chance" positioning for that photograph.

Prayer Experiences

Pray constantly.
— 1 Thessalonians *5.17*

The Lord is near to all who call upon him, to all who call upon him in truth.
— Psalm 145.18

Prayer should not be recited as if a man were reading a document.
— *Jerusalem Talmud, Berakot 4.3*

As a young girl growing up in a remote village in Brazil, I would pray to God to give me a blue-eyed, educated, American as a husband. And my prayer was granted. Now I only wish I had prayed for someone rich and handsome.
— My wife, to everyone

Prayer, the active communication between human beings and some transcendent being, is a practice with a long history. There are written sources to prayer as early as five thousand years ago[26] and some anthropologists believe it was practiced by the earliest *Homo sapiens*. Such communication with a greater power in the universe remains very common in the modern world. Members of such faiths as Christianity, Islam, Judaism, Buddhism, Hinduism, Shintoism, Bahá'í and others all engage in this religious practice, whether privately or communally.

Prayer is based on the belief that not only can the finite communicate with the infinite, but the infinite is interested in and listens to the communication. Furthermore, there is a confidence or hope that prayer may get a response. Countless spiritual texts and personal anecdotes attest to the power of prayer.

Of course, prayer is a practice that is particularly resistant to testing by scientific methods. One could propose doing a double blind study of people praying for others, or for themselves, and look for cause and effect, but it would be meaningless: One cannot control the sincerity of a person's prayer nor expect a Supreme Being to have to answer as if a lab animal with a conditioned response. Nonetheless, at least one such randomized, double-blind, controlled experiment has been done (titled by Richard Dawkins in *The God Delusion* as "The Great Prayer Experiment") involving parishioners praying for patients in distant hospitals—individuals whom they didn't know (they were given the first name and first initial of the last name) and with a prayer that included some standardized content. The experimental (prayed-for) group fared no better than the control (not-prayed-for) group. Which I think surprised no one, neither the religious nor the non-religious, given the shortcomings already noted at the top of this paragraph.

No, prayer remains a very difficult phenomena to study or even conceive a means to study that would satisfy both the Richard Dawkinses and the religious leaders of this world. Experimental designs, surveys, interviews, correlational studies, participant observations—all have their shortcomings. To date, the wealth of data comes from personal testimonies.

The following are three experiences that I had with prayer. Certainly, other people have had far more dramatic testimonies. A Gallup poll of Americans found that about a quarter claimed to have had a vision or heard a voice as a result of prayer.[27] Nonetheless, while my own experiences were more mundane, the first two experiences relayed here were personally life-transforming and the third was an intriguing and difficult-to-explain phenomenon.

Rain

In October 1977, Northern California was in the midst of a major drought, part of the Great Western Drought of '77. Indeed, for California, that year was the driest year in the state's recorded history and the second of two consecutive years of severe drought. Such Northern California communities as Marin, Sonoma, and Alameda counties had mandatory household rationing of water, and people everywhere were being encouraged to save their shower water, share bath water, and engage in other atypical measures to conserve water. "No pull for a pee" became a California quip, and in some places people were turning against each other, reporting neighbors who were watering their lawns at night or surreptitiously washing their cars.

I arrived in northern California that fall as a stopover on a solo journey undertaken after completing my Master of Science degree in Zoology at Pennsylvania State University. I had left home in early August on a kind of American equivalent of the Australian Aboriginal walkabout. While my plan included arriving in British Columbia by September 12 for the Annual Meeting of the American Fisheries Society, my real motive was a kind of spiritual journey, traveling throughout the United

States by myself on a search for meaning. Earlier experiences with meditation has ignited in me a longing to understand about spiritual matters, first through reading books and now through a personal journey.

My quest took me through a lot of varied experiences. By the time I reached San Francisco on the fortieth day of my travels, I had scaled one of the minor Grand Teton mountains, worked as a migrant worker in the apple orchards of Washington State, biked in British Columbia, read about the spiritual phenomena of "soul travel" in a booklet in a Colorado hostel, and hitchhiked through Yellowstone National Park. I stayed in a homeless shelter, camped in a tent, and was welcomed to an overnight stay at a Christian center on the campus of the University of Oregon. A pastor in Washington State, whose job it was to speak to those living in the homeless shelter, was surprised to find my eager, questioning gaze among those sleeping in the pews. However, none of these experiences provided the insights that I sought.

It was while staying in Eugene, Oregon that I felt a compulsion to get to San Francisco as soon as possible, and I headed out in the middle of night to reach my destination. Hitchhiking part of the way, I arrived by bus and soon encountered two women in their twenties who spoke to me about their spiritual community and its openness to the insights from many spiritual disciplines. It was not long afterward that I joined their weekend workshop to the north of San Francisco.

Although I had developed an interest in the general concept of "spiritual matters," that was a far different thing than belief in a personal transcendent reality, a Supreme Being. I was intrigued by spiritual phenomena—I had met someone who had described an out-of-body experience, another who had claimed to have seen spiritual beings, and I myself had mystical experiences during meditation. But a personal God? That was a good way removed from my scientific worldview. Like famous atheists Christopher Hitchens and Richard Dawkins, I had dropped the idea of a personal God as a teenager. And spiritual phenomena themselves, as interesting as they were to read and hear about, surely were explainable as products of matter.

The weekend seminar was not of a general spiritual nature: it was too "God-heavy" for my taste. I attended respectfully, but skeptically, and departed on Sunday, continuing on my journey. But I took a booklet with me to read on the bus ride to Los Angeles. By the time I arrived in Los Angeles, I had finished the pamphlet and felt the insights were worthwhile investigating further. I returned to San Francisco and decided to attend another workshop.

It was during this second workshop, late on a Saturday night, that I decided to take up a suggestion and to privately say a prayer. I hadn't prayed since a youth, and my skepticism remained high. But, what was the harm of offering a simple prayer of inquiry as a test to see whether a Supreme Being really existed and would answer? If I didn't get an answer, I could say that I tried and move on with my life.

And my prayer was just that: a prayer for evidence that God existed. Looking up at the very clear night sky, in the midst of this major area drought, I asked God for rain as a sign. I said that it didn't have be a lot of rain, just some rain. And, to be fair, I said in my prayer that the rain didn't have to happen right away—just by noon of the next day! After all, I was sure meteorological events must take time to develop. It was a sincere and deep-felt personal prayer, the contents of which I kept to myself.

The next day, I arose to yet another sunny, cloudless day. Still time, I told myself. But around 11:00am, as I entered a large, tin-roofed meeting hall for the closing meeting of the three-day workshop, I realized that time had run out. A last glance upward showed not a cloud in the sky.

I remember chuckling to myself that I was free from the constraints that I envisioned belief in such a transcendent reality would entail. I had made a sincere prayer and clearly it was not going to rain. Since it hadn't rained, I was free to do as I pleased.

Then, at 11:55am, as I was standing in the building, I heard a startling sound—the remarkable resonance of rain pattering on the tin roof of the building. It rained strongly, but for only about five minutes and stopped. By the time I had exited the building, the sky was again cloudless, with only the slightest evidence of a rain having occurred.

In the coming days, even hours, my skepticism about the experience being an answer to a prayer would grow. Nonetheless, I realized that the fact that it had rained, so unexpectedly, and had shook me up so much at the time (enough that another attendee expressed puzzlement about my shocked countenance), that I had an obligation to further seek whether God existed or not. I couldn't in all conscience just turn my back on the experience. And the marvelous congruency between this event and my prayer was enough to inform me that my scientific studies, academic inquiry, and objective experimental methods might not suffice as an all-encompassing path to knowledge.

Three dreams

In the summer of 1996, I was confronted with an important decision.

I'd been working with an international nonprofit since 1983. I had a very caring boss, with whom I enjoyed working. I also had relocated my family in 1992 back to my hometown in Pennsylvania, a bucolic, rural environment with extended family, a good school district, and lots of quiet woods in which to enjoy the outdoors. Overall, it was a comfortable existence, complete with substantial personal and professional freedom.

But that summer I was among a select group invited to attend an extended, six-week workshop. The catch was that each graduate would be assigned a leadership role as a missionary in a foreign nation.

The choices confronting me were as different as they were difficult. On the one hand, I felt financially secure, owned a home in a safe area that was also good for raising our young family, and enjoyed my work. I didn't wish to give up that easy, settled life for something unknown. On the other hand, my wife and I felt a certain call, and perhaps conscience-driven obligation, to pursue a more spiritual path of service, one that would be challenging and yet offer unique rewards. I found myself going back and forth. My wife was similarly conflicted and decided to leave the decision up to me. The advice of colleagues and religious leaders was little help: I was getting advice in both directions.

It wasn't a decision we could put off indefinitely. This was a once-in-a-lifetime opportunity with an expiration date, and the time inexorably advanced until the choice had to be made. I either had to depart for this workshop, or I would foreclose the opportunity. Finally, I ran out of time; it became clear that my decision needed to be made by the next morning.

Since I was not getting anywhere with my own internal dialogue, I prayed strongly and specifically that night for a dream to make the decision clear as I slept. I don't recall ever having prayed before for a dream to resolve a question, but I'd run out of awake time.

That night, I received not one, but three very vivid dreams, each with a significant figure in my life of faith providing the same answer. In the first dream, Rev. Sun Myung Moon appeared and counseled me to take the more unsettling path. Then his wife, Hak Ja Han Moon, appeared and likewise counseled me the same. Then, finally, my wife appeared and also indicated that same direction.

There are those who believe the unconscious mind works out problems while we sleep, among other functions attributed to this state of reduced consciousness. Perhaps so. But it is still an interesting phenomenon to pray for a particular dream solution, then have very relevant dreams that are vividly remembered the next day. Regardless, having received the same message from all three remembered dreams, I did go to the workshop (although arriving late thanks to my long indecision). I ended up with the assignment of the Dominican Republic as my new nation, which, being a quick plane-ride away turned out to not require the relocation of my family. It even shared the international calling code of *1* with each U.S. state (meaning one only had to dial the number *1* and the area code of *809*).

With 20-20 hindsight, I can now see that this attending of the workshop was an excellent choice. Furthermore, in an interesting turn of events, within a few months of my decision, events unfolded that would have decisively terminated my so-called comfortable, status-quo option anyway, with the nonprofit for which I had worked effectively closing operations.

The spiritual healing

As a scientist, I still have to think twice, even ten times, before telling the story of a "spiritual healing" that I experienced. To be frank, I'd left out this account in the first draft of this book, since I found it so inconvenient to reconcile with my scientific orientation. And I also knew of efforts at spiritual healing that were widely erroneous—such as the man with an earache who tried a spiritual healing, was diagnosed and unsuccessfully treated, but a medical doctor solved the problem when he found a small pebble had gotten into the ear canal.

Nonetheless, a remarkable concurrence of two proximate events lends credence to my experiencing something unusual.

The issue began when I was working in New York City, and I managed to severely injure my left knee while at a health club. I couldn't walk without significant pain and would hobble down the street, sometimes barely able to get across a city crosswalk while impatient drivers would barrel down on me. For weeks I visited doctors and specialists, had x-rays taken of the knee, went through a series of tests, and tried all kinds of treatments, from warm compresses, to creams, to even acupuncture. Part of the problem was that the x-rays didn't show any structural damage and so the medical community couldn't seem to find a way to solve my pain. It continued unabated, with the same intensity, day after day after day.

My wife suggested a spiritual healer who was reputed to have great success. This woman, Beatriz Steeghs (Gonzales), had grown up among Native American healers in Texas and had spent years counseling people on health and conducting her own spiritual healings. My wife, Lourdes, herself had great faith in healings, since people would come from many miles away to her small hometown in Brazil because of her grandmother's reputation as a healer. However, I was very skeptical, particularly when Lourdes informed me that Beatriz could do the treatment even long-distance from Texas. That had to be one of the most ridiculous things that I'd heard, and I told her there was no way that I would be involved in this.

A few days later, I was hobbling across the city intersection outside my office building in my normal agonizing pain when I noticed the pain rapidly subsiding. By the time I got to the other side of the street, the pain was strangely gone. It was a striking development and a great relief. It had been weeks with nonstop pain.

In a few minutes, I was back in my office, where my wife was also working. I approached her desk to give her the good news. But before I could tell her the pain subsided, ever-faithful Lourdes, in her desire to give me hope, told me that she had good news: she'd gotten off the phone with Beatriz a short while ago and Beatriz already had started "broadcasting" a healing for my knee.

For a skeptic, dealing with confounding variables and selection bias, this is hardly convincing evidence of spiritual healing. But, just maybe the people that traveled long distances to visit my wife's grandmother, and those visiting healers like Beatriz, had greater sensitivity to a phenomenon with at least some validity. For me, the correspondence between the long-distance healing and my own pain abatement was inexplicably stunning.

Spiritual Experiences of Trusted Others

I know a man in Christ who fourteen years ago was caught up to the third heaven—whether in the body or out of the body I do not know, God knows. And I know that this man was caught up into Paradise— whether in the body or out of the body I do not know, God knows—and he heard things that cannot be told, which man may not utter.
— 2 Corinthians 12.2-4

For the core of religion is the twinned principle of arrogance and fear. Fear of oblivion. Fear of an unfair life and an arbitrary universe. Fear of there simply being nothing, no great and grand scheme to existence. The fear, ultimately, of being powerless.
— The Emperor in Aaron Dembski-Bowden, *The Master of Mankind*

Encountering people who profess spiritual experiences is certainly not a rare phenomenon. Glance through the TV channels in the United States and you will find those who claim to communicate with the dead relatives of audience members, while American newspapers, books, and magazines run advertisements about other spiritualists. Drive down American streets long enough and one will see signs outside homes advertising psychics. On the counter of a local Agway store in my neighborhood, among the prices for livestock and pet feed, I encountered a flyer for a mystic who claims she can contact your dead relatives.

The literature from ancient days until the present, from all different cultures and religions, includes testimonies of encounters with God, angels, and such events as faith healing, prophecy, and glossolalia (speaking in tongues). In the book of Luke in the Bible, there is a reference to three of Jesus disciples witnessing Jesus meeting with the deceased Moses and Elijah, and followers of Islam believe that the Qur'an, God's word for humanity, was revealed to Muhammad through the angel Gabriel. St. Francis of Assisi, St. Theresa of Avila, Joseph Smith (founder of the Church of Jesus Christ of Latter-day Saints), scientist Emmanuel Swedenborg, and Rev. Sun Myung Moon offer well-known testimonies of religious experiences with God, Jesus, angels, and/or the afterlife.

Adding to the evidences are such diverse phenomena as out-of-body experiences (OBEs), near-death experiences (NDEs), and channeled works. In OBEs, people report a sensation of being outside their body and sometimes even seeing their own body from such a vantage point. Some reports of OBEs involve individuals traveling to places they have never been and subsequently visiting the locales and finding a match with their OBE experience. In NDEs, individuals who have nearly died, including being resuscitated after being clinically dead, report on experiences they equate with passing into the initial stages of the afterlife. Famous "channeled" works include *Life in the World Unseen*, where the narrator on Earth is an Anglican minister who purports to channel very detailed descriptions of the afterlife offered by "the Monsignor." In *A*

Wanderer in the Spirit Lands, the Italian Franchezzo graphically describes hell.

In the Charismatic/Pentecostal tradition in Christianity, speaking in tongues is commonly practiced, with some testifying to the variation known as xenoglossy, where one speaks a foreign language that he or she has never learned. The modern Pentecostal movement in the United States traces to a prevalence of such phenomena during the Azusa Street Revival, which began in 1905 in Los Angeles, where many of the congregants experienced speaking in tongues, among other spiritual experiences. The ultimate roots for this trace to the Day of Pentecost depicted in Acts 2:4 in the Bible's New Testament, when weeks after Jesus' death, one hundred and twenty believers who were gathered together all began to speak in languages foreign to them.

A 2010 global study of evangelical Protestant leaders, conducted in nine languages by the Pew Forum on Religion & Public Life, found that 61 percent of the respondents claimed to have received a direct revelation from God. Another 47 percent claimed to have spoken or prayed in tongues. [28]

Whatever the source, there is an extraordinary plethora of reports of religious/spiritual experiences, both ancient and current. The question for an inquisitive mind is not the great prevalence of such testimonies; the question is whose testimony does one trust.

Trusted sources

A cynical person might look at first-hand accounts of spiritual experiences as being a collection of bogus reports: from charlatans; from individuals suffering from mental illness or hallucinating from past drug use; from people indoctrinated from youth and influenced by the powers of suggestion; or, a hardwired artifact in the human brain, which once aided human survival but is no longer necessary. Sacred scriptures might appear as no more reliable than ancient fiction—the product of superstitious people unreliably passing myths and hearsay down over the years. The above-mentioned accounts of glossolalia (speaking in tongues), and its variant xenoglossy/xenolalia (speaking a natural language without having learned it), might be treated along the lines of Godlessgeeks.com's seven hundred sarcastic "proofs of God":

#43: Argument from Incoherent Babble
(1) See that person spazzing on the church floor babbling incoherently?
(2) That's how God's infinite wisdom reveals itself.
(3) Therefore, God exists.

#95. Argument from Speaking in Tongues
(1) My friend here once started spontaneously speaking some jibberish that sounded to me kind of like Russian.
(2) But neither he nor I know anything about Russian.
(3) The only explanation is God.
(4) Therefore, God exists.

The fact that certain accounts of spiritual communication have been debunked and various charlatans exposed has added to the natural skepticism. Perhaps the quote above from the fictional Emperor in Aaron Dembski-Bowden's *The Master of Mankind* summaries the view of many—experiences spurred by "fear of oblivion. Fear of an unfair life and an arbitrary universe. Fear of there simply being nothing, no great and grand scheme to existence."

However, much harder to dismiss are reports from people you both personally know and trust. How do you deal with a close, very well-adjusted fellow graduate student who describes her out-of-body experience? What if another respected and stable colleague describes both an out-of-body experience and a vision of seeing Jesus and yet was an atheist at the time? The above-mentioned graduate student, Betsy, was working on her doctorate in biology and was well-steeped in critical thinking. The colleague, Bruce, professed that he honestly didn't believe there was a God at the time of his experiences. Both are honest, sound, sincere, and high-character individuals.

Below I present a selection of testimonies from individuals whom I trust. (Full names will be presented for those whose testimonies have been made public.)

Colleagues' experiences

Numerous individuals, whom I know personally and would certainly say are, by every account, rational, intelligent, and well-respected men and women, have shared profound spiritual experiences over the years. Until my mid-twenties, I dealt with such reports by basically ignoring them: They were too far from my realm of reality to process. An out-of body experience? A report of seeing spirits? Too bizarre to comprehend. Yet, over time, I have heard scores of testimonies of spiritual/religious experiences from people whom I know firsthand and find reliable. In many cases, these individuals weren't even religious at the time of their reported experiences and thus not prone to any associated powers of suggestion. By every measure, these were normal, mainstream, in some cases prominent individuals offering sincere and humble reports that a fair-minded scientist would consider data worth taking into account.

Some of the testimonies involve the intersection of something mystical with a "coincidence." A close friend who would eventually become dean of a college once described to me an experience as a young man leading a team of volunteers in door-to-door fundraising for charity. As he drove through a deserted area without homes or businesses, he saw a strange light encircling the vehicle. It made no sense to drop off any volunteers at this location—there was no one to whom to sell. Nonetheless, the phenomena was so strong that he stopped the van and, in an apologetic tone, asked two perplexed volunteers to start from this deserted locale. Returning later, he found out that they had stumbled across an underground factory, hidden from sight, and had sold out their entire product. I had worked closely with this dean for over two decades on different nonprofit projects and know him to be of impeccable integrity and unassuming nature despite his strong intellect.

Another colleague, Poppy Richie, described an experience in 1972 that greatly altered her career path. A college graduate from a somewhat affluent family, Poppy was actively searching for life's purpose. While in Mexico, she consulted a local spiritualist, who claimed that her deceased mother had a message for her: "You will meet Omma under a full moon by the bay."

One month after the reading with the medium, on September 13, 1972, Poppy met a Korean evangelist named Onni, who, indeed, for years was referred to as "Omma" by those in her church center. (Omma is a rather unusual name in North American culture; but, as Poppy was to discover, it is commonplace in Korean culture, where it means "Mom.") While it was still ten days from a full moon, the encounter took place on the campus of the University of California, Berkeley, located on the east shore of San Francisco Bay. When an American thinks in general of "the bay," it is not uncommon to make an association with San Francisco Bay; indeed, in *Wikipedia* "city by the bay" redirects to San Francisco. The oddity of meeting someone with the rare moniker of "Omma" and doing so "by the bay," prognosticated a month earlier in Mexico, is reinforced by the fact that Poppy worked closely for many years with this woman. Omma, it turned out, was pioneering the development of Rev. Moon's movement in the United States, and Poppy would bring over one hundred full-time members into the movement.

Other colleagues have reported more dramatic testimonies. There was the friend who seemed genuinely stunned one day and haltingly recounted having just seen a person, who was not really there, looking at her as she read scripture. In contrast to this novice to spiritual phenomena, there was the young lady Magdalena, who claimed spiritual openness and one day provided great detail on all the departed souls she professed to be seeing as we walked along the streets of a town in northern California. She described lethargic individuals gathered outside a bar, one departed shouting insults at me, and another swinging fists as if trying to hit my back.

Mark Hernandez, a sincere, humble Mexican-American who grew up in Texas, reported having frequently seen and talked with Jesus since he was young. One of his testimonies is from when he was thirteen or fourteen years old. On this occasion, Jesus came to him and said "I want you to remain pure until further notice." Jesus said that he had a reason for this, and that he wanted Mark to pray about it and to look at the state of the family and the state of world and the state of marriage. Mark said that Jesus added that Mark needed to perfect his brother/sister love before the door to marriage would be opened and that Mark needed first to view every woman as a mother figure, daughter, sister, and grandmother before he would be granted the opportunity to see one as a wife.

Another colleague, Eugene, an America graduate student classmate, could describe in great detail his claimed travels into the spiritual world. Yet another accomplished associate, Perry, provided many testimonies of his communication with the deceased, including those he claimed were hanging around me, providing details of the resentments they were carrying. Perry was by all means a humble and sincere individual, about whom I saw no red flags—up until his out-of-the-mainstream testimonies about the departed.

Those are but a few of many trusted individuals who relayed phenomena that, heard by someone who didn't know them, would cause major apprehension. But there was one individual whose remarkable testimonies I couldn't discount even if I wanted to—Lourdes.

Lourdes

Lourdes deserves special mention, and with her testimonies I will close this book. She has provided me with particularly convincing support for the reality of spiritual phenomena, both for the detail of her experiences and the trust that I have in her. And the trust comes from knowing her well: Lourdes is my wife.

It doesn't hurt that the second testimony detailed below intersected with an experience of my own.

Lourdes is a person of deep faith. Growing up in a strong Catholic tradition in her Brazilian family, she always felt that she had a personal relationship with God and Jesus. Indeed, a repeating vivid dream of Jesus when she was seven and eleven years old, in which she clung to Jesus' robes in the midst of gale-force winds, and a subsequent, life-altering dream of Mother Mary, helped guide her through her youth.

Lourdes had many fascinating spiritual experiences during the time that I've known her. A humble person, she rarely talks about such phenomena. But sometimes I also think that she rarely talks about her experiences because, while many people would find them extraordinary, Lourdes is never awed by them; rather, she treats them as somewhat ordinary. At times, I would only find out weeks or months afterward, and it would require my questioning to pull out the details.

The following are just two of the experiences, selected because I feel they have the broadest appeal.

Christmas angels. Late in 2006, Lourdes had the opportunity to be part of presenting award certificates to prominent civic and religious leaders during an NGO forum. These certificates were not only to recognize the recipients for their contributions to society but also to serve as a commitment to ongoing work toward a world of peace.

However, one pastor declined her certificate, telling Lourdes that she really was hoping that Lourdes could come to her church and present the award in front of her congregation. An agreement was made to make the presentation during that year's Christmas Service.

And this is where a most unusual phenomena commenced. As Lourdes stood on stage, having presented the award to the pastor, the congregation in this Christian evangelical church engaged in unison prayer. Lourdes disclosed that as she glanced up from her prayer, looking out at the congregation, she noticed that angels began to appear in the church, entering in single file and waiting at the back of the church.

One angel, seemingly in the position of leader, approached Lourdes and stood at the bottom of the stage. Without speaking, the angel seemed to Lourdes to indicate that he was waiting for her direction. With her hands and thoughts, Lourdes directed the angels to divide into three rows, with the angles coming down the central aisle and two outside aisles and thus enveloping the congregation. There they remained, not dissipating until the congregation's unison prayer was completed.

Cheongpyeong. Cheongpyeong, or Chung Pyung, is a small town in South Korea, about thirty miles from Seoul. It's located midway between the east and west coasts of South Korea, and at 37.5' north latitude—about the latitude of Athens, Greece, or Oakland, California—it sits not far from the famous 38th parallel that separates North Korea from South Korea.

It is the beauty of Chung Pyung Lake, surrounded by majestic mountains, that has made the town a popular tourist destination during the summer months. Formed where the Hong Chon River converges with the Bukhan River (itself a tributary of the Han River, which flows through Seoul), Chung Pyung Lake has a diameter of almost four miles. It is a man-make lake, created by the Chung Pyung Dam blocking off this North Han River (Bukhangang) midstream. With the green mountains rising up from the water's edge, the traditional Korean homes, and the clear water of the lake and river as it snakes through the mountains, this is a scenic place to visit and to enjoy water sports.

However, in recent years, Chung Pyung has become famous for another feature: the presence of the Cheongpyeong Peace Village, founded by followers of Rev. Sun Myung Moon. At a time when Korea was a destitute nation, still recovering from Japanese occupation and the Korean War, Rev. Moon would go to this area for prayer and meditation. When his ministry was still young, Korean Church leaders would sometimes gather in the mountains for workshops. Then, on July 12, 1971, construction began on the Chung Pyung Spiritual Training Center. This grew into the Cheongpyeong Peace

Village, a large campus with a conference center, graduate theological seminary, hospital, hotel, several schools, soccer stadium, and much more. The impressive Peace Palace towers over the complex, complete with a museum, meeting halls, and residences. By 2011, over one million people from throughout the world were estimated to have visited the Peace Palace and Cheongpyeong Peace Village.

For members inspired by the teachings of Rev. Moon, this is an important holy ground. Both adherents and visitors attend workshops, pray along the paths meandering through the mountains, and seek spiritual healing. Many individuals who visit the site claim profound spiritual experiences.

In the fall of 1996, Lourdes had the opportunity to attend a workshop held in Cheongpyeong. Here she had a number of noteworthy spiritual experiences.

Religious, mystical, or spiritual experiences encompass a wide variety of subjective occurrences, making them challenging for scholars to classify. Some may be indescribable by the individuals or embody non-specific general feelings; others may be specific, detailed, and easily put into words. They may involve perception of events in other places, aspects of other people not normally perceivable (such as auras), and the ability to sense or communicate with people far away or beyond the grave. However, in general, spiritual experiences are considered to be uncommon experiences, which do not fit within the everyday norm and may even evoke fear, trembling, and fascination.

Yet, listening to Lourdes recount her encounters, no matter how stunning they might appear to the listener, makes it seem as if to Lourdes they are wholly unremarkable, ordinary events. I will find myself talking with Lourdes about some issue or person and then she will recount, in a matter-of-fact, oh-by-the-way tone, some event in Cheongpyeong as if she is remembering running into an old acquaintance. Except in her case, the old acquaintance may not even be living on Earth anymore. For Lourdes, experiencing the wholly other is not wholly unusual.

Among the details that I gleamed from Lourdes's experience in Cheongpyeong was seeing her mother daily. Her mother had passed away a few years earlier. Still, Lourdes also longed to see her departed father. But, day after day, for her almost six-weeks in Cheongpyeong, her wish went unfulfilled: he did not appear. Finally, Lourdes reported, on the last full day of the workshop she saw her father, who appeared near one of the trees where she was praying.

But for me the most surprising testimony from Lourdes's time at Cheongpyeong was an encounter that correlated with events I was experiencing in Pennsylvania.

At the time, Lourdes and I were working together in the same office, where she was booking speakers for conferences. One of the individuals with whom we were working was Cheryl Landon Wilson, the step-daughter of the late actor, writer, director, and producer Michael Landon. Michael Landon was particularly famous for his roles on *Bonanza* (Little Joe Cartwright), *Little House on the Prairie* (Charles Ingalls), and *Highway to Heaven* (the angel Jonathan Smith). Cheryl had a compelling story of her time with her beloved father, as well as her own personal exploits, including her struggles as the sole survivor of a car crash that had left her in a coma. Cheryl recounted some of her testimony in her book, *I Promised My Dad*.

In the spring and summer of 1996, some misleading information conveyed to Cheryl by a third party caused an estrangement between Cheryl and my wife's company. Part of the problem was that Cheryl was given a false impression that she was being impacted financially; that if she went with a competitor she could be making more money on each booking. But if that were the only issue it could have been solved with a contract or going separate ways. The real problem was rooted in the strong, personal bond of trust and sisterhood that had developed between Cheryl and Lourdes.

In our office, we recognized that Lourdes, inspired by Cheryl's testimony, had sacrificed bureau profits to help Cheryl. But the disinformation had made it seem the opposite. The misleading information released a deluge of passion in Cheryl that might be compared to a sister being told her own sister was after her boyfriend. Cheryl reacted very strongly. With all the emotion of someone betrayed, Cheryl became very difficult to deal with, as accusations began to fly by mail, phone, and fax machine. Three- and four-page, hand-written letters received via fax from Cheryl was plenty of evidence of the fervor this situation had unleashed in her.

In the midst of this, Lourdes went to Cheongpyeong. Now, the rest of the staff was left with this situation. I dreaded coming into the office, fearing the faxes that would be waiting and the phone calls that would come.

When the situation became overwhelming for our office, I sent a communication to Lourdes in Korea, via a phone message, about the nadir that had been reached, and that we didn't see a path forward. I didn't expect Lourdes could deal with this situation while in Korea—email was still in its infancy and non-existent between Lourdes and Cheryl, and communication via phone from a Cheongpyeong workshop was challenging to say the least— but the situation was so extraordinarily stressful that I reached out anyway.

And then, suddenly one day the hostility ended. Cheryl called to say how delighted she was to be working with my wife's company and hoped to continue working with her. She praised Lourdes to no end, calling Lourdes her sister. It was surreal, but absolutely delightful.

When Lourdes returned from Cheongpyeong, I asked if she had contacted Cheryl while in Korea. She said no, but for me not to worry about the situation with Cheryl, she had solved it another way. I listened spellbound to her account. One night she was praying that Michael Landon could help with this problem with his eldest daughter, knowing how close the two had been. And Michael Landon, who'd died five years earlier, appeared to Lourdes. She explained the need for his aid and got his assurance that he indeed would help. The date when she had this encounter was near the mid-point of the Cheongpyeong workshop—about the same time that the situation with Cheryl inexplicably changed for the better.

This chapter provides but a flavor of the innumerable experiences conveyed to me over the years by not just trusted, but generally accomplished and respected individuals. It goes without saying that I cannot verify their claims: spiritual experiences are uniquely personal. Furthermore, a first-hand account in an individual's own words provides the best data; this chapter chronicles second-hand reports and a limited number at that. What is certainly clear, however, is that such phenomena are neither rare nor geographically limited, and it is likely that many readers have— if not a personal history with such phenomena—trustworthy acquaintances who can add their own testimonies.

Overall, this book enters into the record a number of personal, spiritual experiences that I trust supplements the data on religious phenomena. Ideally, even the skeptical have found it compelling enough to foster an open mind regarding the existence of God and spiritual senses

Notes

1. While Richard Dawkins is widely presented as an atheist, he has been quoted as saying that he self-identifies as an "agnostic," placing himself at 6.9 on the 7-point spectrum he delineated in *The God Delusion*, where 1 is identified as "strong theist," 6 as "de facto atheist," and 7 as "strong atheist." See, for example, J. Bingham, "Richard Dawkins: I Can't Be Sure That God Does Not Exist," *The Telegraph*, February 24, 2012.

2. J. Leake and A. Sniderman, "We Are Born to Believe in God," *The Sunday Times* (London), September 6, 2009.

3. E. J. Larson and L. Witham, "Leading scientists still reject God," *Nature* 398, no. 6691 (1998): 313.

4. M. Stirrat and R. E. Cornwell, "Eminent scientists reject the supernatural: A survey of the Fellows of the Royal Society," *Evolution: Education and Outreach* 6 (2013): 33.

5. D. Masci, "Scientists and Belief," *The Pew Forum on Religion & Public Life*, November 5, 2009; Pew Research Center for the People and the Press, "Public Praises Science; Scientists Fault Public, Media," July 9, 2009.

6. Rice University, "First worldwide survey of religion and science: No, not all scientists are atheists," Pys.org, Dec. 3, 2015.

7. Pew Research Center for the People and the Press, "Public Praises Science; Scientists Fault Public, Media," July 9, 2009; Pew Research Center Religion and Public Life, "U.S. Public Becoming Less Religious: Modest Drop in Overall Rates of Belief and Practice, but Religiously Affiliated Americans Are as Observant as

Before," July 9, 2009; Pew Research Center Religion & Public Life, "When Americans Say They Believe in God, What do They Mean," April 25, 2018.

8. N. Sahgal, "10 key findings about religion in Western Europe," Pew Research Center, May 29, 2018; Eurobarometer Poll 2010.

9. Ariela Keysar and Juhem Navarro-Rivera, "36. A World of Atheism: Global Demographics," in *The Oxford Handbook of Atheism*, ed. Stephen Bullivant and Michael Ruse (New York, NY: Oxford University Press, 2017). ISBN 978-0199644650.

10. Eurobarometer Poll 2010; Study by *Norwegian Monitor* reported in *The Local* (May 18, 2016)

11. Stephen Hawking, *Brief Answers to the Big Questions* (London: Hodder & Stoughton, 2018).

12. P. Davies, *The Mind of God: The Scientific Basis for a Rational World* (New York: Simon & Schuster, 1992), 227.

13. Ibid., 228-29.

14. See, for example, the cases of other scientists listed in Davies, *The Mind of God*, 227.

15. M. A. Thalbourne and P. S. Delin, "A New Instrument for Measuring the Sheep-Goat Variable: Its Psychometric Properties and Factor Structure," *Journal of the Society for Psychical Research* 59 (1993): 172-186.

16. Patrick McNamara, "Precognitive Dreams," *Psychology Today Online Blog*, July 30, 2011, https://www.psychologytoday.com/us/blog/dream-catcher/201107/precognitive-dreams (accessed May 30, 2020).

17. D. J. Bem, "Feeling the future: Experimental evidence for anomalous retroactive influences on cognition and affect," *Journal of Personality and Social Psychology*, 100, no. 3 (2001): 407–425.

18. D. Radin, *Entangled Minds: Extrasensory Experiences in a Quantum Reality* (New York, NY: Paraview Pocket Books. 2006).

19. D. J. Bierman and H. S. Scholte, "Anonymous anticipatory brain activation preceding exposure of emotional and neutral pictures" (Paper presented at the meeting of the Parapsychological Association, Paris, France, August 2002).

20. C. Honorton and D. C, Ferrari, "Future telling": A meta-analysis of forced-choice precognition experiments, 1935–1987," *J Parapsychol.* 53 (1989): 281–308.

21. M. Ullman, S. Krippner, and A. Vaughan, *Dream Telepathy: Experiments in Nocturnal ESP*, 2nd ed. (Jefferson, NC: McFarland, 1989).

22. M. A. Thalbourne, "A Brief Treatise on Coincidence," *Parasphychological Association* (January 9, 2006).

23. Ibid.

24. W. F. J. von Scholz, *Der Zufall: Eine Vorform des Schicksals*; see also L. Browne, "Examining Coincidences: Towards an Integrated Approach" (doctoral thesis submitted, The University of Queensland, 2013).

25. While founded by Rev. Sun Myung Moon of the Unification Church, the Unification Theological Seminary offered an interdenominational graduate-level instruction, embracing the study of a wide range of religious traditions, including Christianity, Judaism, Islam, Buddhism, Hinduism, Taoism, and so forth. Students, at least when I was there, had the opportunity to study under scholars belonging to many different faiths.

26. F. J. Stephens, *Ancient Near Eastern Text* (Princeton, NJ: Princeton Univ. Press, 1950).

27. T. M. Luhrmann, "When the Almighty Talks Back," *Wall Street Journal*, April 5, 2012.

28. Pew Forum on Religion & Public Life, Global Survey of Evangelical Protestant Leaders (Washington, D.C.: Pew Research Center, June 22, 2011).

About the Author

Frederick A. Swarts, Ph.D., has had a distinguished career in the fields of science, education, and nongovernmental organizations. He currently serves as Adjunct Associate Professor of Sustainable Development for the University of Bridgeport, Academic Dean for Bridgeport International Academy, and Life Sciences Editor for New World Encyclopedia. He is a member of the U.S. Department of Energy's Central Institutional Review Board (CDOEIRB) and serves on the board of the Values in Knowledge Foundation.

Previously, Dr. Swarts held positions as Assistant Secretary General for the World Association of Non-Governmental Organizations, Secretary General of the World Conference on Preservation and Sustainable Development in the Pantanal, and Secretary General of the International Conference on Agriculture and the Environment in the Paraguay River Basin. He presented the Keynote Address for the Society of Wetland Scientists 1999 Annual Conference, organized a panel on The World's Fresh Water & Wetlands in the 21st Century for the State of the World Forum, and organized and headed a fact-finding tour of American and international authorities to the Pantanal area of Mato Grosso do Sul, Brazil.

Dr. Swarts is a Phi Beta Kappa graduate of Bucknell University, with a B.S. in Biology, and holds a graduate degree in Zoology from Pennsylvania State University, specializing in aquatic ecology. He completed his doctoral studies at Columbia

University Teacher's College and the Graduate School of the Union Institute, graduating with a Ph.D. in Biology and Education from the latter institution. Among his research endeavors has been an extensive field study of brook trout in streams affected by acid-mine drainage, a study of an exceptional tolerance of some tropical blackwater fish to low pH, and a comparative study of the presentation of evolution in secondary school textbooks of the United States, China, and the then-U.S.S.R.

Dr. Swarts is the editor of *The Pantanal: Understanding and Preserving the World's Largest Wetland*, the most comprehensive, English-language text on the Pantanal region. He is also author of *The Spiritual Code: The 12 Invisible Laws That Govern Our Universe*, and co-editor of *Culture of Responsibility and the Role of NGOs*. He has published scholarly articles in the fields of aquatic ecology, environment, evolution, and education, including in *Ecology*, *Journal of Research in Science Teaching*, and *Transactions of the American Fisheries Society*.

Under the pseudonym Richard Straws, he is also the author of fictional works, including the Hugh Holiday series.

www.ingramcontent.com/pod-product-compliance
Lightning Source LLC
Chambersburg PA
CBHW072100290426
44110CB00014B/1755